NEWSPAPERS
A CENTURY OF DECLINE

NEWSPAPERS
A CENTURY OF DECLINE

How the Internet was the
Last Straw for Print News

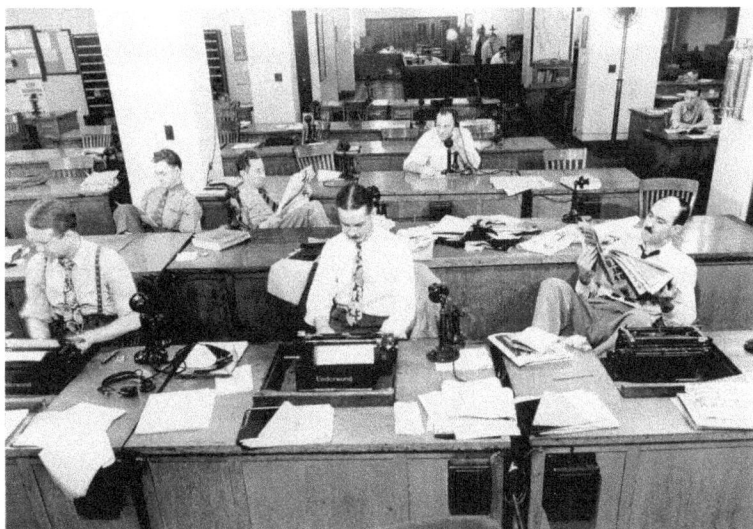

ROBIN BROMBY

Highgate
PUBLISHING

HIGHGATE PUBLISHING - SYDNEY

Highgate Publishing
Sydney

NEWSPAPERS: A CENTURY OF DECLINE. How the internet was the last straw for print news

First published 2016 by Highgate Publishing, P O Box 481, Edgecliff NSW 2027, Australia.
E:info@highgatepublishing.com.au

www.highgatepublishing.com.au Copyright © Robin Bromby 2016

National Library of Australia Cataloguing-in-Publication data
Creator: Bromby, Robin, 1942- author.
Title: Newspapers : a century of decline : how the internet was the last straw for print news / Robin Bromby.

ISBN: 9780992595647

Notes: Includes bibliographical references and index.
Subjects: Newspaper publishing–History.
Newspapers–History.
Online journalism.
Digital media.
Journalism–History.
Press–History.
Dewey Number: 070.5722

CONTENTS

'Why buy a newspaper when you can get your news for free on your phone?'

—Comment posted on the BBC website's report of the closure in 2016 of the short-lived London daily, The New Day. This is a question that remains unanswered.

'By ploughing journalistic resources into online content to the detriment of the traditional print project, as is undoubtedly happening, the industry is effectively cannibalizing itself. It's like a trapped animal that tries to free itself by gnawing off its own leg.'

—Karl du Fresne, former editor, The Dominion, Wellington, New Zealand, 2013.

'We missed the boat not charging for digital. Once people expect to get something for free, it's hard to change'

—Warren Buffett, interview USA Today, 26 May 2016.

Remember when newspapers looked exciting – and they seemed to have plenty of interesting content that was competing for your attention?

AUTHOR PAGE

Robin Bromby has been a working journalist since 1962, in which year he joined *The Dominion*, the morning newspaper in the New Zealand capital, as a cadet reporter. His newspaper career ended in 2016 when his weekly business column in *The Australian* newspaper was the victim of yet another round of cost cutting. Between those two events, he worked for the *South China Morning Post* in Hong Kong in the mid-1960s (which also involved writing for the company's afternoon paper *China Mail* and its *South China Sunday Post-Herald*). Then it was back to *The Dominion* and its then latest creation, *The Dominion Sunday Times*.

Since moving to Australia he worked at The Herald, Melbourne's now former afternoon broadsheet, and the Sunday tabloid (but upmarket) The National Times, and then on to a nineteen-year stint at The Australian (followed by nine years of being a contributing writer there). In between various stints he worked for radio and television news and ran a small book publisher outfit—and also worked both part and full time as a freelance, writing for a variety of magazines including Country Life, Sight & Sound and New Society (in Britain), industry newsletters in the United States, and even a feature for a horse racing newspaper.

He now writes books in the popular history category published via Amazon.

PREFACE:
THE PRESENT PLIGHT

DIGITAL STRATEGIES ARE SUPPOSED to be the newspaper industry's lifeline and future. So how's that going?

Well, as a 2016 a research paper showed, over the previous eight years the websites of fifty-one major American metropolitan newspapers had not, on average, seen any appreciable gains in online readership—this, mind you, when print sales were continuing to drop. The research paper was called 'Reality Check: The Performance Gap between U.S. Newspapers' Print and Online Products, 2007-2015', written by H. Iris Chyi, associate professor at the School of Journalism, University of Texas at Austin, and a doctoral student there, Ori Tenenboim.

They rightly highlighted the fact that 'industry discourse often focuses on the loss on the print side without critically examining the performance of the digital products'. This discourse emphasizes that newspapers have not yet figured out how to monetize online news use, implying that a solution will emerge in the future, a critical point and one that seems at present to be far from resolution. Newspaper companies boast they are on the right track to achieve this nirvana of a future supported by paywalls, but the evidence so far is unpersuasive.

Chyi and Tenenboim note (as will be examined in subsequent chapters) that the decline of circulation has been going on since 1950—although my case is that newspapers were having troubles long before that.

The authors produce some sobering figures. In the years 2010 to 2014, U.S. newspaper print advertising revenues fell from $22.8 billion a year to $16.4 billion. Digital ad revenue increased from $3 billion to $3.5 billion. So as of 2015, the 'dead-tree edition' remains the cash cow, generating eighty-two per cent of revenue for the industry. By 2015 more-over, more than 450 U.S. newspapers charged for online content–an aver-age collect among all those newspapers being $7.8 million. Hardly rivers of gold! Some papers would be picking up just a fraction of that average: according to this study, Gannett's eighty-one local dailies attained merely 65,000 digital-only subscribers as of June 2013. (As this book was being completed, *The New York Times* reported its quarterly results for April-June 2016. Print advertising revenues were down by 14.1 per cent–not surprising as that is the industry trend–but digital advertising revenues were also down, in their case by 6.8 per cent; that is not meant to be the way it should be working.)

And penetration is hardly something to write home about: across the fif-ty-one newspapers studied, the print edition reached 28.8 per cent of local adults, while the online edition reached ten per cent. (The authors chose the papers on the basis of their having circulation of more than 120,473, ranging from *The Orange County Register* with sales of 793,582 to *The Hartford Courant* with sales of 120,473.)

The conclusion by the authors is damning: 'Twenty years into the experiment, the supposedly dying print product still reaches far more readers than the supposedly promising digital product in these newspa-pers' local markets. Print readership is ageing and declining, yet the lack of online readership growth indicates that newspaper readers did not drop print in *favour of* the same newspaper's online edition'.

There is a similar story in Britain, it seems.

The *Daily Mail* is probably the most read online newspaper site, with fourteen million people coming to it each day, a 550 per cent increase in seven years. Yet the 1.7 million print readers each day produce revenues for the publishing company of £499 million a year compared to the £73 million generated by advertising on the website.

As Warren Buffett rightly says, people have become used to getting their news free, and are no doubt outraged when they are expected to pay or are blocked by a paywall. The problem now is that, however much news-paper companies may have come to regret their initial decisions on digital strategy, there is no easy way to unscramble the omelette. This probably explains why so many newspaper managers are publicly so bullish about the digital side: they cannot afford to admit that it has not turned out quite the way they had hoped.

***

Also in 2016 the Reuters Institute for the Study of Journalism surveyed 56,000 news 'consumers' in twenty-six countries. In no English-speaking country were more than ten per cent of respondents prepared to pay for news online; indeed, in the United States, the past year had seen that figure drop from eleven to nine per cent. In Britain it stands at just seven per cent of people reading news prepared to pay for online services.

Then there is ad-blocking; the institute found that this technology is used more widely by people under the age of thirty-five and people who use the news most.

So this does not seem like a recipe for success for digital newspapers.

The record of the past ninety-six years, as charted in this book, does not exactly fill one with confidence as to the ability of newspaper managements to survive this battle. After all, no other industry has been quite as devastated by the digital disruption as have newspapers.

But, as I will argue, the industry has had its back to the wall since 1920 when radio news first hit the airwaves, and then was under siege over many decades from a combination of new technology (television, for example) to the fact there were too many newspapers and too many badly run ones.

Nevertheless, in most cases the print business far outweighs online in terms of newspaper revenues. Present day newspaper managers would be wise to make print work for as long as possible.

INTRODUCTION

"Because of radio, the future of the press is in the air."

–H V Kalterborn, associate editor, *Brooklyn Daily Eagle*, 1923.

ON 2 NOVEMBER 1920 Pittsburg radio station KDKA–which would claim that, on that day, it had become the first licensed commercial station to come on air in the United States–broadcast the results of the presidential election between Warren G. Harding and James M. Cox. About 1,000 people listened to the radio broadcast. The station had made an arrangement with the morning daily, the *Pittsburg Post-Gazette*, to be supplied with the results as they came in during the evening. Those 1,000 people were the first in Pittsburg to learn that Harding had won: they did not have to wait for the thud of morning newspaper at their front door the next day.

That broadcast signified the first dent in the monopoly held on the news by newspapers. It was but the first crisis; in 1922, only one American household in 400 had a radio but by 1933 radio was being listened to in more than sixty per cent of American homes. There was also another challenge, one that affected evening newspapers but not so much the morning ones. Long before television dealt most of the afternoon dailies the final, telling blow, those titles were faced with a new logistical problem: traffic. The growing number of motor vehicles clogged roads in cities, meaning afternoon newspapers had to bring deadlines forward to allow for delays in distribution. That gave radio another edge. (It also led some newspapers to stop distributing papers to the outer parts of their circulation areas, another bunch of readers lost.)

It has been a prime example of what might be called a long Darwinian struggle: first radio, then television; then competition in print from suburban and regional weeklies (and suburban dailies in the case of American papers) and direct mail advertising. None of those adversaries also had to wrestle with a legacy of over-manning, expensive distribution systems and hikes in newsprint costs (in the case of weeklies, hikes in newsprint prices mattered far less to them than to a seven day a week operation that was printing perhaps half a million copies a day rather than the weekly's print run of, in many cases, just several thousands).

Even as early as 1967 *Time* magazine was lamenting of newspapers that 'in the past, the fight was for larger circulation gains; now much of the struggle is just to keep from losing readers'.

Now, several crises later, newspapers have faced the worst of all those crises, the media equivalent of the hospital superbug and, as a result, many titles have already succumbed while for others survival chances are doubtful; and this latest threat is one so great that it is increasingly held as self-evident that newspapers are finished—if not immediately, then within a few years. The internet and digital news services are widely expected to see them off.

Overall, the Western newspaper industries have seen little or no growth overall since 1970 in terms of total newspaper industry circulation totals. In the United States, that was true even with fifteen per cent population growth over the years from 1970 to 1985 (although advertising overall among American titles rose by fifteen per cent in that period, in what seems now to have been an Indian Summer for the U.S. industry).

It was also the case post-1970 that some newspapers were able to enlarge their reach. By 1985 *The Wall Street Journal* was being printed at four locations across the country; that enabled the paper to attract advertisers who wanted to reach potential customers in just those regions. The Gannett Company was able to use the new satellite technology to connect its eighty-nine papers in thirty-nine states—and launch *USA Today*, with its colour photography. *The New York Times* was printing in more than one location, including San Francisco and Los Angeles. (But still *ninety per cent* of that newspaper's sales were within a 100km radius of its hometown.)

For the rest of the industry, the news was not so cheerful. And now few newspapers have been left untouched by the internet.

Circulation figures plunge with each new audit, advertising has dried up. Walter Isaacson was managing editor at *Time* when it first went online. In 2009, writing in his old magazine, he ruefully reported that there were two consequences. *Time* invented banner ads that brought in a rising tide of revenue but, in order to get the traffic to justify the advertising, the magazine abandoned charging for content. Secondly, in seeking the easy internet ad dollars by putting content online for free, all those magazines and newspapers that did this found the ad dollars not coming to them but to operations that did not create the content but benefitted from it: search engines, portals and aggregators.

Sydney-based futurist and author Ross Dawson made a splash with his 'newspaper extinction timeline', a chart showing when newspapers in their present form would become insignificant. Papers in the United States, according to that chart, would be insignificant by 2017, in Iceland and Britain in 2018, in Australia by 2022, France by 2029 (although that seems optimistic given French newspaper sales at present). But he had good news for newspaper proprietors in Russia, Mongolia and Argentina: their newspapers would be alive and kicking until 2036, 2038 and 2039 respectively according to the chart. (Certainly it seems his forecasts for the tipping point for US newspapers may have been a little pessimistic And, personally, I think Dawson was being far too bleak in regard to Britain: in 2016, the nationals were going along reasonably well with the exception of the now online only *The Independent*.)

***

Let us have no illusions: we are now talking not just about newspapers disappearing. No, the even more serious threat is that the companies that publish them will consequently be left without a viable business plan. By this I mean: the revenues from digital subscriptions in most instances, if present trends are anything to go by, will never by themselves sustain any large journalism enterprise equivalent to the newsroom of a metropolitan newsroom. Obviously, there will be exceptions as in the case of *The Financial Times* and *The Wall Street Journal* -- but then, anyway, those titles will probably be among the small number of newspapers that will survive in print form. As this book was being written, *The New York Times* announced plans for a global digital reach. There will be other exceptions; but not many newspapers have the reputation or clout that would make such a plan in the least bit plausible. As this was being written, the *Los Angeles Times* announced it was going global in terms of coverage with bureaux in several foreign cities; this followed a plunge into beefing up state and local coverage.

There will be other types of exceptions: the *Christian Science Monitor* survives as a (very good) digital news site eight years after abandoning print, but then it has the backing of the First Church of Christ, Scientist, and it has a reputation built on decades of fine journalism, a quality which it retains online.

And it will help if a billionaire buys a newspaper—although whether that guarantees it staying as a print product, as well as online, in the long run is yet to be seen.

But, for the others, it is hard to see how—or even why—newspapers should prosper in digital form only. Apart from the severely reduced revenues that would inhibit any large spend on newsgathering, by being online only they are on the same playing field as every other website (although the aggregators will take a blow without lifting stories from the newspaper sites!).

That is why I am arguing that newspapers should battle on with print as long as they can. Without print, they are just another website.

Therefore, newspaper companies should be trying as hard as they can to remain just that—newspaper companies, and I will be looking at examples of papers that are making that effort. Digital alone is an escape tunnel that in many cases will lead to a financial dead end. And, at least, when you print a newspaper you keep control of the product; with digital, you have to try and figure out what sort of relationship you can have with Google and Facebook, and who will be calling the tune—and how to protect your material from others.

***

So who am I to be sitting in judgement on what the newspaper industry did wrong (and it did plenty wrong)? I am not a famous or legendary editor, nor a journalism professor.

But did I spend fifty-four years in newspapers (with brief breaks for radio and television dabbling, or writing books). Make that fifty-six years if you count working on the university paper before going into the real newspaper business. By the age of twenty-seven I had risen to be chief reporter (or chief of staff as it is often called) on a metropolitan daily, *The Dominion* in Wellington, New Zealand's capital city (and I later served as deputy editor on its Sunday edition).

But, after 1971, I never held any executive position in the industry. Nor did I switch to deskwork in the editing process, or seek better rewards in public relations. I just liked knocking out stories, as it was termed.

And, from the front line (as it were), I watched an industry change.

I never stopped being fascinated by newspapers. Nor did I cease being disappointed by many of them. When, as happens a couple of times a year, I arrive in Tokyo en route to Europe, the first priority is going to a newsstand to pick up copies of the two English language Japanese papers and the locally printed editions of *The Financial Times* and *The Wall Street Journal*. Now that I am out of the newspaper business, I spend at least two months of any year in Paris—and, there, the first thing every morning is to go out and pick up the London national papers, the *WSJ* and the *International New York Times*. And when I am driving around my home country, New Zealand, I stop at every small town or city that boasts a daily newspaper (including the *Ashburton Guardian* which sells more than 5,400 copies daily in a town of fewer than 20,000) to buy a copy.

So, yes, I am—notwithstanding all the ups and downs of slugging out a living writing from them for all those years—still a newspaper junkie.

Since 1979, I have also worked as a business journalist. As much as any aspect of the newspaper game covered in this book, the business story is a dominant thread.

What I have set out to do in this small work is correct any misapprehension that everything was fine until the internet came along. On the contrary, as you will see, the industry was in trouble before it became possible to update yourself by reading a screen.

This is that story.

***

And yet ...

Amid all the gloom about the future of the newspaper in Western countries, there is one counter-intuitive fact that cannot be ignored: the fact that, at least in the United States, people are lining up to get their hands on newspaper businesses.

There's Warren Buffett, of course; Berkshire Hathaway's BH Media is one of the ten largest U.S. newspaper companies, with thirty-two daily papers and forty-seven weeklies. We have seen other 'outsiders' come into the business: Jeff Bezos of Amazon, sports mogul John Henry and casino owner Sheldon Adelson. In Britain Alexander Lebedev bought *The Independent* and the *Independent on Sunday*. The latter has now disappeared, the former gone digital only.

So it will be interesting to watch whether these outsiders can save the industry, or transform it (the first being highly dependent upon the second).

And then there are the traditional publishing companies sticking by newspapers, most notably the Gannett Co., which is still expanding its business. At the same time as Gannett was making a bid to buy Tribune Publishing, owner of dailies including the *Los Angeles Times* and *Chicago Tribune*, Australia's most venerable masthead owner, Fairfax Media, was continuing to lay off staff at Melbourne's *The Age* and the *Sydney Morning Herald* and to talk publicly about going to Saturday-only publishing, the rest of the week just being digital publishing.

... newspapers can survive

But, in my opinion, the industry needs major surgery. The approach to the crisis in recent years has been less than half-hearted. The default formula has been to put up news on the web, perhaps add a paywall, and hope for survival, while sacking staff, seeing print advertising flee, and not knowing what else to do.

I believe there is a future for newspapers, but not one predicated on advertising revenue. Much of the advertising has already fled, certainly that revenue from the once rich cash flows from classifieds.

To me, it seems the biggest mental stumbling block when dealing with this issue is what is wrong with the newspaper. It is not circulation; that is, fewer people buying papers (although that is a serious problem) but rather the disappearance of advertising revenue. After all, the newspaper industry has historically striven for higher and higher sales to readers in order—primarily—to attract more advertising. It should be remembered that the increasing sizes (in page number terms) of newspapers in the 1950s and into the 1960s were a response to the demand from advertisers for space, not primarily a demand from readers. And the big drives to capture more readers were primarily motivated by the need to show those advertisers that plenty of people were eyeballing their ads.

Now, in a post-print advertising era, you should be able to make money on a circulation of 10,000 as well as with one of a million. So, it will be argued here, newspapers can survive by getting smaller (as well, of course, as revamping their concept of news and feature content, of which more later).

There is another issue: namely, some papers (again, *The Wall Street Journal* or *The Times* in London spring to mind) can draw in big numbers of people who are prepared to pay for their online content. Then there are the others, and that tends to be particularly true of popular tabloids, where people are not prepared to pay for online content. Just look at London's *The Sun*: it erected a paywall when it was selling 1.8 million print copies a day but managed to get only 225,000 people to sign up for its digital content. The paywall was subsequently scrapped.

Readers need motivation (for example, financial interest in keeping up with the markets) to motivate them into shelling out for a digital subscription. But if readers are interested mainly in celebrity gossip, to take another example, the experience so far seems to suggest they will access it only if it is free. So where does that leave down-market newspapers if the print era is on the way out? It will be interesting to watch.

Perhaps we are looking at two different trajectories here. The common factor with the situation in most newspapers is that advertising is drying up. The papers with readers who take seriously the content of what they are reading will likely sustain those publications in some form. But even then the papers will have to be smaller, and the staff numbers also smaller. And cover prices will have to cover most of the costs of producing papers, which means those prices have to rise.

It seems to me that most newspapers are adopting the strategy of seeking survival through attracting more online revenue while slashing costs. But that really is a half-hearted approach. What is particularly frightening is that most industry thinking has stopped at this point. There is little sign that, generally speaking, newspaper managers have grappled with the need to bite the bullet and consider a full transformation of their print product.

It will not be easy or palatable to the industry to tackle that issue. But there seems no obvious alternative; not to face harsh reality will mean the end. Without a print newspaper, there is no reason for a newspaper to exist as anything but yet another website. Companies without a print product are just another website, and the competition is cruel.

But, before we consider the remedy, let us consider how the industry got to this pass—and how the internet was just the last straw.

Karl du Fresne, who once edited the morning daily in New Zealand's capital (Wellington's *The Dominion*)—and whom I first came to know when he joined the paper and worked on my reporting team in the late 1960s—sums up the situation in an article published in 2013 by the *Manawatu Standard* (an afternoon paper located in the New Zealand provincial city of Palmerston North—and still surviving). He wrote the following:

'Newspaper bosses seem to regard increased website traffic as a cause for celebration. In effect, they are applauding their own impending extinction. Here's how I see it: consumers realize they can read content online, often long before it's printed and, not unreasonably, deduce that there's no point in continuing to buy the paper. Sales consequently decline and advertisers respond by pulling out of the paper. But, crucially, those advertisers don't seem to be shifting to newspaper websites, so there isn't enough revenue from the brave new digital world to offset the slump in print advertising. Result: a vicious cycle of steady decline. Am I the only person who sees this as a fatally flawed model?'

The answer to that is: too few in the newspaper industry comprehend the flaw in the model. And that remains the case today.

***

Here's another wrinkle in the story so far, and one pointed out by Nick Cohen, a British author and columnist for *The Observer*. Writing in the monthly London-based opinion magazine, *Standpoint*, he shows how so many newspaper sites that offer free access, and thus have to sell advertising to make money (or contain losses), need to 'strain to attract hits'. And it corrodes a newspaper's image. He cites the *Daily Mail*, a newspaper that has for a century reassured grumpy conservatives that their cause is just. But that conservative content, still alive and well in the print edition, is hard to find on the paper's website. Instead, there is celebrity news, fashion, showbiz stories by the yard, and readers who want the meaty material by the right-wing pundits really have to spend time searching for it. His point is that the *Mail* and other sites can determine what interests particular readers accessing them online and target advertising accordingly; in this instance, the digital tail is wagging the print dog, all in the quest for clicks and advertising pennies.

But he is also concerned that the system turns journalists into thieves and liars. 'To get traffic, fewer and fewer news sites can afford to send out writers to find original content. So they steal from other news sites, or lift and repackage a YouTube video or Twitter exchange that might go viral,' writes Cohen.

Esquire columnist Luke O'Neil fessed up in December 2013. He tells of making a living publishing about twenty-five pieces a week, from considered features to 'tossed-off reaction blogs'. He said his online work involved him in passing along 'some pretty sketchy nonsense' such as a roomful of kids being shown the movie *Nymphomaniac* instead of the Disney flick they were expecting.

O'Neil wrote: 'In order to make a living, those of us who had the bad sense to shackle ourselves to a career in media before that world ended have to churn out more content faster than ever to make up for the drastically reduced pay scale. We're left with the choice of spending a week reporting a story we're actually proud of (as I do just frequently enough to ensure a somewhat restful sleep every other night), reaping a grand sum of somewhere in the ballpark of two hundred to five hundred dollars if we're lucky, or we can grind out ten blog posts at twenty-five to fifty bucks a pop that take fifteen minutes each. That means the work across the board ends up being significantly more disposable, which in turn makes the readers value it less, which means they want to pay less for it, and so on'.

Is that the way newspapers want to go?

***

We must never forget that newspapers do have an appeal that the internet will never have.

In 2014 Matthew Parris, former Conservative member of parliament and columnist for *The Times*, wrote in *The Spectator* magazine about 'the lost pleasures of reading a proper newspaper'. He had established the habit of buying each day a print copy of the paper for which he writes but read all the other titles online. Online for that was 'brilliant', he said; you could dive in and out, click video links, cover a range of papers in a few minutes if you know what you were looking for, and so on.

But then he had boarded a two-hour flight out of Liverpool bound for Barcelona and, to switch off, bought a newspaper, then once on board ordered a cup of tea and decided he would relax with the paper.

It dawned on Parris that you could do something with a newspaper that you cannot do with a computer or Smartphone: relax. He read all the columnists, including one who had included a moving poem, all the letters to the editor 'even one about rugby which was very funny though I'm not interested in rugby. I learned from a nature diary that lichen is not an organism but a partnership of algae and fungi. A colleague had written feelingly about the death of his mother'. Then Parris read all the coverage of a political crisis in the Labour Party.

Upon landing, and folding away his newspaper, Parris reflected that he had just read a paper just, as once, we all used to do. 'And I had realised that I was missing something: something that had slipped away while I wasn't looking,' he ended.

And there's another thought: perhaps most of us are just too busy to read newspapers anymore.

1. FORGETTING THE FUNDAMENTALS

Every time a newspaper dies, even a bad one, the country moves a little closer to authoritarianism; when a great one goes, like the *New York Herald Tribune*, history itself is denied a devoted witness.

–Richard Gluger, Pulitzer Prize winner

BY THE TIME THE internet threat arrived, the newspaper industry was in no shape to compete or fight back. The newspaper model was already broken and no one was doing much about it; or, at least, no one was doing *enough*. The problem was that no one had done enough about the mounting problems for the industry–or, at least, found a way to reshape the industry to halt the decline, much less to return it to its past glory–since radio first set up in competition in 1920.

KDKA had become the first licensed station in 1920 when it took to the air (although there had been many unlicensed broadcasters before that). By 1922 the United States had six hundred radio stations on air. *The Detroit News* was the first American newspaper to start a radio station. However, early newspaper-owned stations were not seen by their proprietors as independent media outlets; rather, they were regarded as a means to promote the newspaper titles, with news bulletins used as teasers to motivate listeners to go out and buy the paper to get the full story. In the same way, some newspapers had their popular columnists read some news items, or sections of their columns, over the airwaves. In 1923 there were in the United States eighty-four radio stations owned by newspapers.

Yet by 1924, newspapers had closed or sold some of these stations; the broadcasting units were seen as costing too much for the perceived return. (That view would soon reverse itself once the advertising revenue streams were established in radio; by 1929 the newspapers owning radio stations included the *Chicago Tribune*, the *Chicago Daily News*, the *Kansas City Star*, the *Milwaukee Journal*, and the *New Orleans Times-Picayune*. By 1937, of 689 stations across the country, 194 were newspaper-owned—and seen as media enterprises in their own right. In Australia, too, newspapers wanted to get into the radio business; under Keith Murdoch—father of Rupert—the company that published Melbourne's afternoon broadsheet, *The Herald*, bought station 3DB in that city; the owners of the *Sydney Morning Herald* similarly took a stake in Sydney station 2GB.)

But the trend was not the newspaper industry's friend.

In 1923, before radio had made any severe inroads, 503 American cities had two or more separately owned newspapers; by 1972 only forty-nine cities were in that category—and twenty-two of those cities had separately-owned papers but were working with joint business and printing arrangements. Between 1970 and 1980, newspapers in America's twenty largest cities had lost twenty-one per cent of their collective circulations.

As Leo Bogart chronicles in his 1982 study of the newspaper in transition (see bibliography for details), the postwar years had seen newspapers try to fight television by running bigger photographs, along with more features and personality journalism. Indeed, the *Miami News* had billed itself as 'the newspaper for people who watch television'. (That title folded in December 1988.)

Yet other strategies also failed. The afternoon *Minneapolis Star* folded in 1982, the title being merged with the morning *Tribune*. Its circulation by then had fallen from 300,000 to about 170,000. Rather than fight for life by billing itself as a newspaper for people who watch television, the *Star* cut back on reporting daily news in favour of long, analytical articles. The publisher, Donald R. Dwight, acknowledged that this had not been a way to attract the younger and more affluent audience the paper had seen as its road to survival. The death of the *Star* left only twenty-nine American cities that could boast of having two separately owned and competing newspapers; there were, by contrast, 128 cities that had two newspapers still, but in all these cases they were either jointly owned, jointly operated or shared presses.

And switching from afternoon to morning publication, or giving the impression of that by afternoon newspapers turning out editions all day, did not work either, as in the early 1980s such papers as *The Washington Star* and *The Bulletin* of Philadelphia had learned to their cost. Interestingly, the former did not die because of lack of lack of readers, but the shriveling of advertising revenues; the latter was battered by an invigorated morning competitor grabbing the greater share of advertising in that market.

Until 1920, newspaper circulations (as a whole, and at least in the United States) had been growing more quickly than the population. Radio did for that trend. And the advantage radio had over newspapers was eerily similar to the edge taken by the internet eighty years later: radio could provide news and information far more quickly (no waiting for the newspaper delivery trucks to battle through the traffic to your local newsstand or news-agency store, and then further time while the paper boys did their rounds). On top of that, radio was free to the consumer. And, for many advertisers, radio was a more direct and cheaper way to reach potential customers; readers of newspapers could quickly flip to the next page, but listeners had to endure the advertisements that dotted programming.

And now ad-blocking applications means the newspaper industry faces a threat to what advertising is left.

Paywalls? Yes, they work for some. But readers can usually find most of what they need for free and so bypass the sites guarded by paywalls (unless you really did need specific formation). Websites can get news up in minutes (although many are still too slow). And for advertisers, the internet is cheap: no four of five figure sums that need to be spent to run a full page advertisement. (And, as this was being written, there were reports that digital advertising rates were falling over many categories.)

Again—and using the United States as the leading example, both because of its free enterprise system in place when radio began (as opposed to state control in many other then developed countries) and also because Americans have documented this field in much more detail than other countries—there are similarities between the response by newspapers in the 1920s to radio's threat and present day tactics with the internet.

As I will show in the following pages, newspapers have been under threat, to some degree, since 1920 when radio arrived on the scene. But that was only the first of a succession of such threats. And the industry really did not reform itself in any meaningful way. In 1950, *Time* magazine described one aspect of self-indulgence, the newsroom at *The New York Times*: 'The *Times* city room is one of the world's biggest: forty yards wide and a full city block long ... Reporters are usually summoned to the city desk by a public-address system. From his desk at the south end of the city room, Turner Catledge (the executive editor) occasionally uses a pair of binoculars to see which reporters are in at the north end. In this sea of faces (some 300 altogether, including copyreaders, assistant editors, re-write-men, etc.), many a young reporter's talent often tends to drown'.

I bet it did. Here, by contrast, is a newspaper where the editor needed no binoculars. This photo was taken in 1968 at *The Dominion Sunday Times* in Wellington, New Zealand, on which this writer was a reporter (one of three in total).

This is the paper's entire full-time editorial staff. The newspaper had a national circulation and the staff consisted (from left) of Jack Kelleher (Editor), Graham Billing (seated, reporter), Robin Bromby (standing, reporter), Neil Anderson (sub-editor), Frank Haden (chief sub-editor, and later editor), Barrie Watts (reporter and columnist), George Taucher (compositor; he had all but the Saturday news and sports pages ready for press by Friday evening) and Paul Taylor (sub-editor). There were two part-timers (a South Island correspondent and the editor of the children's page) and the woman's section—yes they existed back then—filled one fashion page each week). On Saturdays additional sub-editors from the daily, *The Dominion*, were brought into help with production (and, of course, the typesetting and composing rooms were fully staffed), but otherwise the team in the photo was pretty much it. All three reporters wrote several news stories and features each week, both under their own bylines and as 'Sunday Times Reporters' or 'Special Correspondent'—we tried to look a bigger outfit than we really were—while Watts also was the main columnist and this writer was the book reviewer (under yet another pseudonym). Then three years old in 1968, the Sunday edition was experiencing rapid growth; true, one reason is that the circulation area was expanding as more areas of New Zealand were supplied with the newspaper, but also the Sunday paper was alone in doing what newspapers do best, breaking stories and putting time into investigative journalism, which made it a noticeable standout among a largely docile daily press in New Zealand at that time.

Could you run a national weekly on this type of shoestring operation today? Why not? We did not have the internet; we used telephones and jumped on buses to go see interviewees, overseas features were sourced from London's *The Sunday Times* (owned by the same company, and sent by air express, the editor clipping articles from the pages and sending them off to the typesetters), and the three reporters managed not only to fill the newspaper every Sunday but to break stories that the supine dailies avoided, or simply did not look for.

Even with all the staff shedding of recent years, daily newspapers need substantial staffing levels to write and produce those daily editions. And that, in many cases, is no longer sustainable. But weeklies—and here I am thinking mainly of Saturday-only or Sunday-only papers—may be a plausible halfway house on the road to extinction.

As I will conjecture later, it may be necessary think about what amounts to shoestring operations, as one part of a total re-think of what newspapers are. One of those aspects is the actual size of the newspaper (do they need to be that big—after all, they expanded in postwar years to accommodate the flood of advertising?); another is the pricing. Newspapers have depended on advertising to cover a greater or lesser proportion of their standing costs, and so see the cover price as topping up the ad revenue. Could smaller papers (total page numbers, that is) and a higher cover price work? After all, building circulation was done mainly to tempt advertisers to take space, to reach a greater number of readers. If there is little advertising to be won, why lose money on every copy you sell?

***

'It's not an audience problem – it's a revenue problem,' said Larry Kilman of the World Association of Newspapers back in 2011. His case was that plenty of people may not be *buying* newspapers but plenty were *reading* newspaper content on web and mobile devices. As we know, newspaper companies have finally woken up to the need to charge for content; but even now many still do not. Even for those who do it seems unlikely to work to the extent of replicating and replacing the revenue streams that once came from print advertising; those traditional revenue streams have largely gone, or at least are in the process of going. Can web and mobile device traffic replace the 'rivers of gold' of classified advertising, or of full-page retail advertisements? If they cannot, then newspapers will not be able to exist as they are, employing sufficient numbers of reporters to find and break news stories, and employing experienced sub-editors and editors to make informed assessments of the quality the copy reporters and feature writers turn in.

There is no alternative: concentrate on the main product (the print newspaper) because, without that, there will be no business. It may not work; indeed, if the trend in the developed world is any guide, it will not.

But the worst thing would be to give up on the print model as the foundation stone of any newspaper business without trying something new. The 'something new' so far has been to surrender to the internet; newspapers offer all sorts of incentives to those taking out online subscriptions (up to and including handing out tablets to those subscribing). But what incentive do they offer those who trudge out each day and hand over coins for a print copy of the paper but are not particularly interested in also having an online subscription? Or who commit to having the paper thrown over their front fence each morning?

No: 'something new' has to be a total rethink of the way in which newspapers are run and edited. Tinkering with what is essentially a century-old approach is doomed to failure to judge by how newspapers are faring at present. (True, I have no magic solution. In a later chapter I will outline a few thoughts on how to plug at least some of the holes in the hull of the slowly sinking ship but someone needs to come up with a brand new design—and pronto.)

Newspapers have become so transfixed by technology they have neglected their fundamentals. So you have newspapers offering gadgets as a reward for taking up digital subscriptions. If the digital side of the business was replacing (pro rata in terms of costs) what was lost from the print side, then, yes, try and get everyone to go digital. But the digital side—with a few exceptions such as *The Financial Times* or *The Wall Street Journal*—is a pale shadow of what print used to be as a revenue generator.

Mark J. Perry of the University of Pennsylvania, writing on the American Enterprise Institute website, shows that U.S. newspaper advertising revenues, when adjusted for inflation, have fallen from $67 billion in 2000, to $38.15 billion in 2008, to $16.4 billion in 2014. Even when, to that last figure, you add 2014 digital advertising income, it totals just $19.9 billion. Also adjusted for inflation, newspapers are now attracting fewer advertising dollars than in 1950, the point at which postwar revenue from this source began a huge and long climb.

Warren Buffett's 2007 pronouncement that the economic potential of a newspaper internet site 'is at best a small fraction of that existing in the past for a print newspaper facing no competition' is pretty much true today as it was when he spoke those words. Take an Australian example: Fairfax

Media, which publishes the *Sydney Morning Herald*, Melbourne's *The Age* (and their Sunday equivalents) and the national *Australian Financial Review* (along with a host of Australian regional newspapers and several daily newspapers in New Zealand) in 2015 reported its first revenue rise in four years. That rise amounted to a one per cent increase; its new business areas, including digital news, were by then contributing to the 'turnaround'. But, at the same time, revenue from its metropolitan papers fell seven per cent and its regional papers by eight per cent (although nothing can be extrapolated about the viability of some types of local papers from that latter figure as this division ranges in size from bigger regional dailies, such as Dubbo's *Daily Liberal*, to small town weeklies such as the *Milton Ulladulla Times*). A tiny gain like that is hardly the 'rivers of gold', the term coined by Rupert Murdoch for Fairfax's once famous (and now largely gone) revenues from classified advertising. Talking about platforms is fine, but that is only one problem when newspapers are having multiple organ failure.

Staff cutbacks have been savage in many newspaper companies. Well, given the state of the industry's revenue flows that is not surprising. But, just to make matters a great deal worse, too often the surviving staffers now increasingly resemble battery hens, locked to their desks turning out instant news stories for the paper's internet site, then writing a version for the print paper that will probably say little different to that which appeared the day before for digital subscribers.

In May 2016 Fairfax Media in Australia showed more staff the door, many of them senior, experienced writers, cartoonists and editors, including the *Herald's* economics editor, its main business investigative writer, its investigations editor, Asia-Pacific editor and property expert writer. Mark Day, media column writer on *The Australian* (and a former newspaper editor), summed up the Fairfax situation: 'Fairfax will be left with younger, cheaper reporters who will be judged on their ability to generate online clicks,' he wrote. 'Gone are the concepts of news breaking, journalistic rigour and values.' It should be added that Day, even though writing in a Rupert Murdoch-owned newspaper that is a Fairfax competitor, has long been generally even-handed in his treatment of non-Murdoch media.

Day acknowledged the great standards that once applied at Fairfax. (And

I should add here by way of testimony that I once wrote for *The National Times*, the Fairfax weekly that lost money for years but was supported for the depth and breadth of its journalism; my first major assignment on the paper was a profile on a well-known business figure and being given five weeks to research and write the piece; imagine that these days!) As Day said of Fairfax, 'it is indisputable that good content has been the driver of newspaper sales for generations ... Newspapers still make up the majority of Fairfax's revenue and profits, so why on earth would management seek to destroy that in a seemingly headlong rush to a digital-only future where click-bait reigns supreme?' Why indeed?

Too many newspapers got away with mediocrity for years because there was no alternative. In fact, in an almost bizarre mutation of Darwinism, the disappearance of many of the weakest papers gave the survivors a false sense of security, especially in those places that became one-newspaper towns. Sure, the surviving titles grew fat on the monopoly of print advertising–those big ads listing all the supermarket specials, the car dealer advertisements, properties for sale and apartments to let, along with the listings for local cinema programs–but too often management rested on the oars.

Papers were in trouble across America, and still no internet in sight.

On 31 December 1938, *Editor & Publisher* was bemoaning that costs in newspaper companies had grown substantially over the preceding twenty years and 'tend to freeze themselves into the newspaper structure. They do not fluctuate with the rise and fall of income'. It was this situation that was leading to a growing number of cities with only one daily newspaper.

Union regulations had taken their toll, but it was the paper and raw material costs that had killed off many newspapers. Advertisers bought space on the basis of circulation (the equivalent of present-day clicks) and had little patience with the claims of quality editorial content. Retail merchants wanted to limit their spending to one newspaper; they would 'rather pay one advertising bill than two or three', noted *Editor & Publisher*.

Then there were the newspapers that were badly conceived, or could not be saved. In 1921 a group of businessmen began a second afternoon newspaper in Melbourne, Australia, in competition with the deeply entrenched *The Herald*. By the time they closed it in April 1925, the *Evening Sun* (which was printed on pink paper) had lost somewhere between £200,000 and £300,000, a fabulous sum at the time. A statement announcing the end complained of the mounting costs of raw materials, the continuous expansion of wage sheets, the unavoidable high costs of speedy distribution. Even the legendary Australian newspaperman Keith Murdoch had his failures, as when he tried to revive the ailing *Adelaide Register* in 1928 by smartening up news coverage and dropping the cover price, but it closed in 1931.

Of course, the Great Depression hurt newspapers everywhere. American newspapers in total earned $797.3 million in advertising revenue in 1929; by 1933 that stream of cash had fallen to $428.7 million, and by 1937 had still not recovered to pre-slump levels, advertising bringing in $574.2 million that year.

The slump aside, newspapers would continue to be under pressure from a combination of changing market conditions, growing competition, rising costs and the failure of the papers themselves to produce editions that satisfied buyers.

In 1956 Louis B. Seltzer, editor (1928-1966) of the afternoon daily *Cleveland Press*, was featured in a *Time* magazine report headlined 'The Press: What's Wrong?' Seltzer's view was that newspapers had gone flabby: magazines were by then doing the in-depth reporting while newspapers were beefing up with 'fiction, features, crossword puzzles, panels, columnists, comics and other entertainments' and, on the news front, were just going through the motions waiting for press releases to arrive. And here we have, all of sixty years ago, Seltzer urging newspapers to tackle colour printing so as to compete with magazines and television. Yet it took them decades to react to the challenges to their circulation and advertising bases from those other media. And, when they did, too often they aped Andy Hardy: whenever (in the Andy Hardy movies starring Mickey Rooney and Judy Garland) the teenaged couple faced what seemed an insuperable problem, the solution inevitably was 'let's put on a show'. With newspapers it was 'let's put on another lifestyle section'.

At the same time, papers were out to lunch on the subject of their main news content. Mark Ethridge, publisher of the *Louisville Courier-Journal* (a paper that, fortunately, is still with us now), in 1958 complained that the falling circulations of many newspapers was the fault of those newspapers themselves. He said there was too great a reliance on syndicated leaders (editorials) and on syndicated columns, and to the running dull and slanted press releases as news. Other criticisms heard at that time related to the poor coverage of local news, and reluctance to run crusades against social problems such as slums. When profits fell, too often the first management reaction was to cut editorial costs. Sound familiar?

Or how about the relevance today of this comment on the American press in *The Economist* on 28 April 1958: 'Editors and reporters are no longer fired by the traditional ambition to get all the news first and best or perish in the attempt. The profession has become stale, stodgy and standardized ... Hard-hitting crusades, outspoken comment and three-dimensional reporting that pulls no punches are seldom found in the newspapers, unless they are dealing with shocking conditions far from home and retaliation'.

In the late 1950s, few American papers could compare to Fleet Street on the basis of sales. One of the exceptions was New York *Daily News* with a circulation of 2.1 million (3.85 million on Sundays). Even the mighty *Chicago Tribune* in 1958 sold just 954,000 copies on weekdays, while *The New York Times* managed daily sales averaging 557,000 (although that doubled on Sundays). Unlike Britain, there were substantial newspaper chains, the largest being Scripps-Howard with twenty-two dailies and Hearst Corporation being second placed with fifteen dailies; one out of every four newspapers was run by a chain.

There was another response to falling or stalled circulations that became almost a kneejerk reaction to any decline in circulation: 'Let's redesign the paper'. This comes into the 'If I had a dollar for every ...' category. Finding it too hard to figure out a better content strategy? No problem, let's pay a designer to mess around with the type face, leave more white space (none of which the average reader ever notices) or move the crossword or drop a comic strip (which the reader sure *does* notice).

In 1977, with circulation falling fast, the owner of the afternoon *Chicago Daily News* decided on a redesign of the newspaper and to introduce more features that would appeal to younger readers. The title folded on 4 March 1978. The paper had been in existence for 102 years and was the first daily in the United States to post foreign correspondents abroad.

(*The Chicago American* succumbed in 1974, leaving the Windy City just two dailies, the *Sun-Times* and *Tribune*–in a metropolis that had once boasted fifteen dailies).

But the *Daily News* is another illustration of the main theme of this book: that the industry had plenty of shortcomings long before the internet came along. There were, as with any sector of private enterprise, those companies that did not get the product right. Ten years before the *Chicago Daily News* closed, *Time* magazine (in a survey of the Chicago newspaper scene) opined that, for all the talent on its editorial team, 'since the 1950s it has not been able to come to any useful conclusion about what it wants to be'. It had tried being a quality newspaper, then it strove to attract readers with more middle-of-the-road fare. Neither worked. In 1967 it announced a plan to project more 'warmth and informality'. Then, as we have seen, ten years later the ploy was to gain young readers. Those latter initiatives were as successful as the preceding ones.

Newspapers have, of their own volition, decided to dump readers who might have bought a newspaper mainly because of some specialist section. Once regular columns on subjects like stamp collecting, gardening, chess were common features in newspapers. I recall back in the 1980s when riding in a Sydney taxi finding a young driver with a copy of *The Australian*, the national broadsheet and a relatively earnest paper. So I–being a reporter on that newspaper at the time–began asking him a few questions about why he bought the paper. It turned out that, of all the newspapers in the city (two broadsheets, three tabloids), *The Australian* was the only one that printed the fields for horse race meetings across the nation, as opposed to those just for meetings in their own state, and therefore was a must-buy for that dedicated punter. Editorial teams often forget that people buy newspapers for a variety of reasons, and not always for the latest political exclusive, the opinions of highly paid columnists, or in-depth features.

In early 2015, *The New York Times* dropped its thrice-weekly bridge column and Friday movie theatre listings, a decision brought about by further budget cuts. The bridge column's disappearance brought 2,500 letters of complaint from readers. One such letter cited sections and features disappearing without forewarning; after all, there's nothing that quite annoys long-standing readers (and obviously older ones) than familiar parts of their newspaper suddenly one morning no longer being there. Another letter noted that 'soon the obits will disappear and we won't even know if we're dead or alive'. Others pointed out that many older readers (the folks who still buy papers) depended on the movie listings in the newspaper as those people preferred letting their eyes wander down a column of print on paper to searching online. In reporting on this issue, the paper's Public Editor, Margaret Sullivan, noted that 'all of this comes in the context of *The Times* reinventing itself from mostly a print newspaper to mostly a digital news and information company. It's a very tricky transition since most revenue still comes from print but the future is certainly digital'. Good luck with that.

Here is another example of how to annoy readers. In June 2016 the *Otago Daily Times*, a morning broadsheet in Dunedin, New Zealand, had its sports editor responding to a letter complaining about the dropping of the regular previews of the city's premium football league by saying that the premier league preview could not be included because there was a lack of space. To this explanation another reader wrote: 'In the next Saturday's paper after reading this letter (and the sports editor's reply) I noted half of the back page was taken up by a photo'. Yes, you see, the readers do notice these things. Memo to layout people: you cannot compete with television with huge pictures; you can compete with television by running information that readers enjoy and find useful.

So there we have it: annoy the older readers, and perhaps have them cancel their subscriptions, while not replacing them because newspapers are not attracting younger readers. It would be hard to find anyone that would dispute that. Yet, as reported by *The Financial Times* in January 2015 in a full-page study of the book industry, 'the endurance of physical books has relied on young consumers'. Overall, it seemed by the beginning of 2015, e-book and e-reader sales had reached some sort of plateau and physical book sales had resumed growth. In the United States in 2014 adult fiction physical book sales had fallen eight per cent but sales of young adult fiction rose twelve per cent. The paper quoted Paul Lee, a media analyst at Deloitte, thus: 'Print newspapers are resilient among those who have grown up with print newspapers. Physical books are resilient among all ages'.

Clearly these younger readers buying physical books enjoy the content of the books they buy. But, also clearly, they are not interested in what is in newspapers. The demographic clock is ticking louder and louder with the death of every older regular newspaper reader. Yet here is something that puzzles me: I happen to live in an inner suburb of Sydney, one that has the largest remaining concentration in the world of Victorian terraced housing which the locals wearily feel is the renovation capital of the world. Each morning hordes of tradesmen arrive in the area for the continuing stream of renovation projects and many of their vehicles have on the dashboard a copy of Sydney's morning tabloid, the *Daily Telegraph*, with its usual shock-and-awe front page headline and lashings of sport. The majority of these tradesmen are younger men, certainly aged in the twenties and thirties, but these young men are still reading a newspaper every day. That rather goes against the received wisdom. Perhaps here's one newspaper that is producing content those younger readers *will* read.

In January 2015 the world followed the *Charlie Hebdo* story; on 7 January two gunmen from an Islamist terrorist group shot dead eleven staffers of the French satirical magazine and wounded others. The story of *Charlie Hebdo's* sales pattern is well known; the magazine had previously struggled on sales of around 30,000 a week. The first post-killing edition saw almost eight million copies sold. By mid-2015, the magazine had managed to solidify its base at around 200,000 prepaid subscriptions.

But the story that concerns us here is what *Charlie Hebdo* meant for Parisian newspapers. A good deal, it seems. By March Celestine Bohlen was reporting in *The New York Times* that the *Charlie Hebdo* tragedy had boosted sales of national newspapers (and usage of their websites, it must be conceded) as the French sought reliable, in-depth updates of the developing story; here the key word is 'reliable' because, for all their faults, newspapers are edited with facts checked; with the web, who knows? *Libération* saw its sales double (to more than 62,000 copies—which in itself is a comment on the state of French newspapers, given Paris has a population of 2.24 millions, and France sixty-six millions). *Le Monde*, *Le Figaro* and *Le Parisien* also had substantial sales boosts. Those papers' websites saw hits rise around sixty per cent. The report quoted Jean-March Lepine, owner of a news and stationery store in central Paris, saying his customers turned in those terrifying days to newspapers whose credibility and analysis they knew they could trust.

A year and a half later, the world watched Brexit, the United Kingdom voting in favour of leaving the European Union. The vote's result brought about the resignation of the then prime minister, David Cameron, who had nailed his colours to the 'remain' mast. Newspaper sales in London soared in the days after the dramatic turn of events. *The Times* claimed to have sold an additional 100,000 copies on the Saturday (up eighteen per cent) and *The Guardian* saw a twenty per cent gain to 70,000. Even the *Daily Mirror*, not a title that one would immediately turn to for the most commitment to serious political coverage, put on an extra 40,000 sales. *The Daily Mail* moved an extra 90,000 copies and *The Sun* 52,000. In fact, total sales for the British national newspapers were up 724,000 across three days.

When they have something that is of importance to people on their pages, then people will buy newspapers. That is surely a ray of hope.

Online traffic rose, with *The Guardian* website (free) seeing a record seventeen million visitors the day after the Brexit vote.

But here's the question: we know, both with the French and British examples, that the newspapers would have made extra revenue from the newsstand sales of the printed product, but did they make anything *significantly* extra from all those additional clicks?

NINETY-SIX YEARS
OF CRISES

New York is the capital and crossroads of the world's press. No papers anywhere gather and print more straight news than the morning *New York Times* and *Herald Tribune*. The tabloid, comics-choked morning *News* has the largest daily circulation (2,007,797) of any newspaper. The conservative *Sun* and its afternoon feature-story rival, the *World-Telegram*, are commuters' specials. And there are half a dozen other papers not counting *The Bronx News*.

Time magazine, 5 October 1942

WHEN IN 1928 ORSON Welles and his Mercury Theatre colleagues broadcast the radio dramatization of H.G. Wells' science fiction story *War of the Worlds* regarding an invasion of aliens, and created panic among those listeners who had tuned in after the opening disclaimer, there was one interesting side story that throws some light on the state of the newspaper industry.

The morning after the broadcast Welles appeared at the headquarters of the Columbia Broadcasting System to face the press. In his recent biography, *Young Orson*, Patrick McGilligan recounts of that press conference that 'for a decade, newspapers had gradually lost ground to radio in both advertising revenue and timely reporting ... Among the old-school newsmen there was a distinct "anti-radio" sentiment, as *Variety* notes in its account of the broadcast and the panic, and this in turn lent an anti-Orson slant to the press conference.'

(The book, covers in great detail Welles' theatrical ventures and quotes reviews from local papers; the names include the *New York World Telegram*, the *New York Herald Tribune*, the *Evening News* – all but a memory today.)

Back in 1920 when station KDKA signaled that the days of papers' monopoly on news was at an end by broadcasting the result of the presidential election hours before the morning newspapers could be delivered to homes or newsstands, the observer of the newspaper scene could have been forgiven for thinking that broad sunlit uplands lay ahead of the newspaper industry.

At the annual meeting in London of Associated Newspapers held in 1922, the chairman was able to boast that the *Daily Mail* had a larger net sale than any other daily newspaper in the world; the *Evening News* had a larger net sale than any other afternoon newspaper. Of the *Over-Seas Daily Mail* he was able to boast that it 'increases its popularity throughout the British Empire and is highly appreciated by advertisers who wish to cultivate the growing markets of the Dominions (Australia, New Zealand, Canada, Newfoundland, South Africa and the Irish Free State)'. That year the company had launched an Atlantic Ocean edition of the *Mail*; the large Cunard liners plying between England and the United States printed a version of the paper each morning, the content compiled from news sent by wireless from New York and London.

Another London paper, *The Sunday Pictorial*, was by 1925 selling an average of 2.13 million copies a week. The paper had been launched on 14 March 1915 and, on that first day, achieved sales of more than one million copies. At the 1925 annual meeting, chairman John Cowley had this to say: 'Today we regard the Sunday newspaper as a necessity for Sunday reading and enlightenment and it is difficult now, after ten years, to imagine what our Sundays were like prior to 1915, when no such thing as a Sunday illustrated paper existed'.

The next year *The Daily Chronicle* began printing in Leeds as well as London to build circulation in the north of England and in Scotland. However, its fortunes were soon to change; in 1930 it was forced to merge with *The Daily News* (the newspaper founded in 1846 by Charles Dickens) to become the *News-Chronicle* (which survived until 1960).

But these seemingly good times were not to endure and, even then, there were plenty of newspapers in trouble. In 1922, for example, the afternoon papers in Detroit (the *Detroit Journal* and *Detroit News*) sought survival through merger.

The First World War was a boost to the fortunes of British newspapers, but before 1914 many newspapers closed, their deaths caused partly due the rise of Northcliff's *Daily Mail* (founded 1896) which made some of marginal papers unsustainable (especially after the *Mail* opened a printing plant in Manchester to increase its circulation outside London), and also C.A. Pearson launching the *Daily Express* in 1900 with a cover price of a halfpenny. Once the war, and the demand for news about the conflict, was gone London papers began failing, including the *Daily Chronicle*, the *Pall Mall Gazette*, the *The Globe* (started in 1803, in 1921 it was forced to merge with the *Pall Mall Gazette*) and, in 1937, the last edition appeared of the *Morning Post*, a newspaper title that had been founded in 1772.

The past ninety-six years have seen recurring newspaper crises. Sure, this one is different and, unlike earlier ones, the electronic-cum-cyber revolution does have the strength and impetus to finish off large numbers of newspapers in the coming years. That said, newspapers have been failing for more than a century. Radio was the first electronic threat that affected the newspaper industry with little discrimination. The next wave, television and its evening news caused mass casualties among afternoon (sometime called evening) papers.

Yet even before radio, the newspaper business was beset by problems. In the early years of the twentieth century, Frank A. Munsey made himself the most hated man in the news business when he figured there was one major problem: far too many newspapers were competing for the finite numbers of readers and the amounts of advertising available; and so he proceeded to close one title after another. That there was a limit to the number of readers and advertising dollars available was underlined in 1931 when

Herbert Pulitzer and his two brothers sold off their late father's three newspapers in New York—the *New York World*, *Evening World* and *The Great
Sunday World*. Herbert Pulitzer said the problem was that New York had
too many newspapers, ten dailies based in Manhattan alone with another
four in Brooklyn (and that was without counting the daily financial and racing sheets).

Not that New Yorkers—and the people of the then developed countries—were slouches when it came to buying papers. Figures produced in
late 1923 showed the *New York World* selling 382,739 copies a day and
the *Evening World* another 272,335. (Nor had Joseph Pulitzer been reluctant to keep up with technology: the New York World in 1896 became the
first newspaper to have a four-colour press—although it does raise the question, to which we shall return, as to why it took many decades on for colour
printing in newspapers to become commonplace.)

The biggest seller of 1923 was the New York *Daily News* with 633,578
sales, followed by William Randolph Hearst's *Evening Journal* (601,837).
The New York Times sold 362,361 copies each day followed by the *Evening
World* (no figure found), on to Munsey's *Sun* and *Globe* (236,165), the
Evening Mail (170,327), then two other Munsey papers, the *New York
Herald* with 165,710 buyers and the *Evening Telegram* with 133,230,
and lastly the *Evening Post* with a circulation of just 32,506. (I have also
not been able to find a circulation figure for the *New York Tribune*, which
would merge the following year with the *Herald* to become the now famous
New York Herald-Tribune.)

It might seem that having three papers, morning, evening and Sunday,
as Pulitzer did, might seem to make for a stronger entity. In this case it did
not: Pulitzer found that advertisers wanted to spend only in the biggest selling publication and were reluctant to add outlays for the other two.

***

(A digression, but one with a purpose: it was Pulitzer's *The Great Sunday
World* that was the first true Sunday nespaper. For five cents, the buyer
received the first newspaper consisting of multiple free-standing sections,

including fashion, comics, puzzles, sport. In a review of a 2005 book on graphic art in that Pulitzer Sunday newspaper, New York novelist and feature writer Kevin Baker said the magazine and humour sections set a whole new standard:

From them pour forth one sumptuous, antic, multi-colored spread after another; not only a slew of very eccentric, very funny editorial cartoons and comic strips, but also breathless features that celebrate nearly every marvel of the age–from robber barons to Arctic explorers, bathing beauties to new immigrants; and bridges, and world's fairs, and subways, and skyscrapers, and airships, and the most amazing new phenomenon of them all, Teddy Roosevelt.

Later in the review, Baker asks a pertinent question: all of this raises the question of why the papers today, and all other news media, are so drab by comparison–a point worth pondering.)

The Pulitzer sons in 1931 were faced with losses over the previous five years totaling $5 million and had only enough cash, some $400,000, to continue publishing for another three months. The papers were sold to Scripps-Howard; the morning and Sunday editions were scrapped and the afternoon paper folded into the Scripps-Howard *Evening Telegram* to become the *World-Telegram*.

***

Munsey became so hated because he closed so many newspapers–seven in New York alone, during his career. He closed the *Daily News* in 1904–no connection with the one founded in 1911 as America's first tabloid–and then merged *The Press* and the *Morning Sun*, and later merged that title with the *Herald*. His *New York Mail* was merged into the *Evening Telegram* (the one later owned by Scripps-Howard) and the *Globe* with the *Evening Sun*. He killed Philadelphia's *Evening Times*, too, and he sold off or merged others, including Baltimore's *Evening Times*, the *Boston Journal*, and the *Washington Herald*. As George A. Douglas explains in his history of the newspaper industry's golden age, 'Munsey was not wholly mistaken about what was wrong with the newspaper field'. Many of the bigger cities had a dozen or more English-language dailies. 'Many were struggling gamely along with their own individual charm and distinction, but they were chasing readership that was not out there', Douglas added.

That, alas, is the story applying to many newspapers down the ages.

***

The internet was still a long way off in 1982 when newspapers were already dying –not the industry (yet), just individual papers not strong enough to hold on. In September 1982 the *Buffalo Courier-Express* printed its last edition after 146 years in existence after a five-year battle with the *Evening News*. At the time the *Evening News* was selling 264,000 copies compared to the sales of 127,000 by the morning paper. The *News* immediately introduced a morning edition. Investor Warren Buffett had bought the afternoon paper in 1977 and soon after the *News* introduced a Sunday edition that established sales around 200,000 and cemented its superior revenue stream.

But economic problems went even further back. In 1958 the *Washington Post*, one of many newspapers that had been hit by rising postwar cost increases, lifted its weekday street price to ten cents. The price had last been raised in 1944 (to five cents) but in the following fourteen years the cost of newsprint and wages had almost doubled. In 1958 the afternoon newspapers in New York had lifted their cover prices but their circulation numbers took such a hit that the morning papers held off following suit.

According to *The Economist* in 1958, few metropolitan newspapers were in good financial health. *The New York Times* depended on a newsprint subsidiary to provide half its earnings; the newspaper industry as a whole had seen its share of advertising revenue decline steadily since 1949 when television stations began to open in large numbers. The big papers also suffered from the opening of suburban newspapers that took a share of both readers and advertising. The magazine cited the case of Long Island's *Newsday* that had built a circulation of 269,000, largely at the expense of the New York dailies.

Then there were newspapers that could have survived longer but were closed for other reasons. One such case, which this writer experienced at close quarters, involved a New Zealand provincial morning paper, the *Manawatu Times*. It was located in the city of Palmerston North, 145 km from the nation's capital Wellington. In its local area, the *Times* was in competition with *The Dominion*, the morning daily based in Wellington (at which at the time I was a junior reporter); The Dom, as everyone called it, regarded the lower half of the North Island as its territory, and relied heavily on sales out in the regional areas because its circulation in Wellington itself was much lower than that of the afternoon paper, *The Evening Post*, with its dominance in both circulation and advertising (both classified and display). In the late 1950s the *Manawatu Times* had been losing money, but by 1963 was again in the black. In a move that shocked both the public in Palmerston North and the staff on both newspapers, The Dom's owner, the Wellington Publishing Company, bought the *Times* on one day and closed it the next. The move did boost the Wellington paper's circulation but soured its reputation, especially in the *Times*' area. (*The Evening Post* outlived many afternoon dailies, surviving until 2002, at which time it was merged with the morning paper, which became *The Dominion Post*.)

But, generally, it was shrinking or disappearing margins that did for papers. (And, I have to remind readers again, that this was long before the internet as we know it came into being.)

In 1974 the Beaverbrook newspaper empire in Britain was losing large sums of money. If you think things are pretty brutal in the newspaper industry now with all the retrenchments, consider the first week of April in 1974. At a stroke, the Beaverbrook management shuttered its print works in Glasgow, abolishing three newspaper titles—the *Scottish Daily Express* (circulation 577,000), the *Scottish Sunday Express* (500,000) and the *Glasgow Evening Citizen* (151,000). In all, 1,800 employees were out on the street without jobs. The villain in this instance was the soaring cost of newsprint. (There is always something going wrong in the newspaper industry it seems.) In those days so great was the dependence on advertising to keep newspapers profitable that an economic downturn, leading to a fall in advertisement bookings, could quickly make a paper unprofitable.

In 1992, still before the internet grabbed the newspaper industry by its throat and began the slow strangulation, Anchorage, Alaska, lost one of its newspapers, the *Anchorage Times*. According to an assessment by *The New York Times*, the Alaskan daily was for most of its life the dominant journalistic voice in Alaska 'but it failed to adapt to changing times and competitive pressure' after the Californian-based McClatchy Newspapers (owner then of the *Sacramento Bee*) in 1979 bought the *Times*' competitor, what was described then as the 'anaemic' *Anchorage Daily News*. At the time of that purchase, the morning *Daily News* sold just 11,500 copies a day, compared to the afternoon *Times*' circulation of 45,600. McClatchy poured big sums of money into its acquisition and rolled out a new Sunday edition. Six years later the *Anchorage Daily News* was the top selling title. The *Times*, which had missed the opportunity years before to switch to morning publication, closed in 1992.

By the early 1980s the United States had forty-nine cities that still had at least two separately owned newspaper titles. In 1923, there had been 503 such cities. During the time America was at war, 1941 to 1945, 130 per cent of households took a newspaper; in other words, many households were buying two or more newspapers each day; this penetration had been cut in two by the 1990s.

By the mid-1960s—more than thirty years before the industry began to feel the full impact of the internet—the newspaper business was no longer a race to beat competitors and build circulation; no, now the fight was to save readers from deserting newspapers. Over the first six years of that decade, Chicago's four dailies (*Chicago Tribune*, *Chicago Sun-Times*, *Chicago American* and *Chicago Daily News*) between them lost more than 115,000 copies sold each day.

In 1945, New Yorkers still had the choice between eight dailies, Bostonians not far behind with seven papers from which to choose. There were five dailies in Chicago, four in San Francisco. By 1982 the newspaper world had lost the *Philadelphia Bulletin*, the *Minneapolis Star*, the *Cleveland Press* and others.

One market that experienced newspaper rationalization in a matter of just two years was Sydney, Australia: at the beginning of 1988 it had six daily newspapers: in the mornings, there was the *Sydney Morning Herald*,

The Daily Telegraph, *The Australian* and the *Australian Financial Review* (the last two being nationally circulated); in the afternoon there were two tabloid titles, *The Sun* and the *Daily Mirror*. On Sundays local readers had had the choice of four titles, the *Sun-Herald*, the *Sunday Telegraph*, *Sunday*–formerly the *Sunday Mirror*–and *The National Times* (for its few last years it was renamed *Times on Sunday*). But then change came quickly: by 1990 the two afternoons had disappeared and two of the Sunday papers went as well.

There was no internet in April 1979 when Associated Newspapers, publisher of London's *Evening News*, revealed it was making staff redundant, dropping the Saturday edition, and reducing from seven to four the number of editions on weekdays. Newspaper companies have typically been reluctant to face the cold hard facts. To their credit, most have persisted with their newspapers even when the writing was on the wall. In the case of the *Evening News*, by 1979 it was making a loss of £7 million a year. Then management laid out a plan to axe a large number of the 2,300 people (yes, 2,300) on the payroll, eliminate the Saturday edition and reduce from seven to four the number of editions on other days. The unions fought, naturally, but here's the thing: even after all those cuts, it was predicted the newspaper would still lose money, at an expected £2 million that year.

Take France as another example of pre-internet decline. In 1972, Paris' newspapers were suffering from what was described in *The Irish Times* as falling or stagnant circulations throughout the 1960s (after a 'golden age' in the 1950s). The biggest blow was the introduction in 1968 of commercial television in France. Newspapers had already been facing 'a heavy burden of taxes, distribution costs, higher salaries and production charges'. Some were kept going by more profitable divisions of their own companies; in the case of *L'Auraure*, a conservative daily, it was able to survive only because of the profits earned by the popular horse racing paper owned by the same company. *Paris-Jour* was supported from the revenues of its owner's stable of romantic magazine titles. According to the same report in *The Irish Times*, the newsprint costs consumed all the fifty centimes that readers paid to buy a copy of *Le Figaro* in the 1960s; fortunately the paper was still then thick with advertising, that source contributing eighty per cent of the title's revenues–but that advertising bonanza did not last much longer.

In 1988 *Le Matin de Paris* folded because, as *The Economist* put it, 'it was not much good and because there are no longer enough readers to go around'. At that time—again, in the late 1980s and before the internet became a news source—the eleven dailies in Paris either lost money or made pitifully small profits. It appears that the situation as observed in 1972 by *The Irish Times* still held true: while *Le Figaro* sold 420,000 copies a day in 1988, it was said to survive mainly because of the glossy magazines it included with the paper at weekends.

(Actually, *The Economist* report did not explain the full story of *Le Matin de Paris*. In his 1998 book on the French press, Clyde Thogmartin explains that the newspaper was founded in 1977 and within three years it had achieved a circulation of 200,000, a sales figure it had taken competitor *Libération* some twenty years to achieve. He describes the paper as 'strong in cultural news, a feature that helped it develop a following among traditionally left-leaning French schoolteachers', not a demographic that would immediately commend itself as the basis for a newspaper business plan.)

In 1982, while charting the decline in newspaper titles up to that time, the general manager of America's Newspaper Advertising Bureau, Leo Bogart, declared that 'the "worst" appears to be over'. For all the losses in readership, circulations appeared to have stabilized over the previous five years, he noted. Bogart believed newspapers would survive into the twenty-first century but wondered what they would look like. (Unfortunately, apart from colour printing and fewer advertisements, not all that much different, which is part of the problem.) Yet he took great heart from the fact that while, in 1980-81, twelve daily papers folded (including the *Washington Star* and *Cleveland Press*) twenty-five new ones were started.

In 1982 the *Los Angeles Times*, under a headline proclaiming 'Papers are Becoming Part of the Gloomy News They Report', said that declines in advertising volume, particularly in classified advertising, had squeezed profits at many of the nation's 1,730 dailies. Newspaper industry unemployment had more than doubled in the past year (to 34,000 in the second quarter of 1982). The then financial recession had seen *The Wall Street Journal* experience a twenty-nine per cent drop in classifieds in June 1982 alone.

The writer of the article, Bill Sing, noted the experience of three report-ers from the *Washington Star* after that paper closed. One got a sports writing job at the *Baltimore News-American* but was laid off after less than two months when that paper undertook massive layoffs (the title would die in 1986); another landed an editing job at the *Minneapolis Star* but then received a pink slip when his new employer merged with the *Minneapolis Tribune*; the third, Annamarie deCarlo, did better in that she lasted a whole year at the *Escondido Times-Advocate* until she again was laid off. Today, alas, there is nowhere to go for newspaper people laid off.

A more recent example, illustrative even though it involves a magazine, was *Ladies' Home Journal*: it still had some 3.2 million buyers in 2014, but advertising had halved between 2009 and 2013, and then fell a further twenty-two per cent in the first quarter of 2014, at which stage the owners decided they could no longer sustain monthly publishing. It continues as a quarterly, newsstand-only magazine.

The *New York Herald-Tribune* suffered from a double-whammy: it died in 1966. The paper had been losing readers and advertising because it was unable to attract sufficient numbers of advertisements; but then it was struck by a four-month long strike by ten unions that destroyed any chance that, if publishing resumed, readers and advertisers could be wooed back in sufficient numbers.

And, in the case of the smaller dailies in particular, television (and then the internet) robbed them of much of their news. One of the obvious moves was to drop international coverage. Take the *Kenosha News* in Wisconsin in 1915. It may have featured local stories on its front page (road improve-ments and local baseball matches) but further inside its readers could catch up with the fiasco of the Dardanelles, the latest position on the Hungarian front, or Japan's part (on the side of the Allies in that conflict) in the world war. More and more smaller dailies abandoned this coverage as the bigger newspapers penetrated into their circulation areas and then, after 1945, television provided the average person with a world view through nightly news broadcasts.

***

'Print is not dead' is a chapter subtitle in *Out of Print*, by George Brock, professor at the Graduate School of Journalism at City University London. (He had also been a working journalist, including being foreign editor at *The Times*.) His argument is that print is not dead, nor will it die, but rather that it is the business model for newspapers that is the problem. He goes on to say books, directories or magazines will not necessarily go under even if newspapers do. He makes the further point that, over the five years to 2012, circulations in Western Europe and North America had fallen by seventeen per cent. By contrast, newspaper sales in Asia had risen by sixteen per cent over the same period. What it comes down to, in Brock's analysis, is that print is indeed not dead—but that applies mainly to Asia when it comes to newspapers.

But he makes another valid point (and this goes back to my earlier points about the redesign default position—don't make the content better, just make it prettier to look at). Brock cites cases in the British nationals of format changes. The *Independent* and *The Times* went to tabloid, *The Guardian* to the hybrid 'Berliner' size halfway between tabloid and broadsheet. These changes gave the papers temporary appeal but, says Brock, 'once the effect of the novelty had worn off, the deeper trends reasserted themselves and the circulation declines continued'.

***

There were times when it seemed that the newspaper golden era still existed. In 1927, newspapers in the United States saw a surge in circulations. *The New York Times* remarked that the industry was benefitting from 'an unusual number of important news events, improvement in the quality of newspapers, a widespread growth in popular education, an extension of interest on the part of newspaper readers, and a growing practice of reading from three to five newspapers a day instead of one' was seen as combining to get people buying more papers, although Ralph Pulitzer of *The World* attributed the rise in his paper's sales to dropping the cover price from three cents to two cents. But it is true that papers had much to report that year, and radio was not able to provide the necessary breadth of coverage; in the

1920s there had been the Mississippi floods, Calvin Coolidge announcing he was not going to run for a second full term as president, the Lindbergh flight across the Atlantic and the Sacco-Vanzetti murder trial. J. C. Dayton of the *New York Evening Journal* said competition had made publishers improve their newspapers and distribution systems. J.M. Patterson of the *Daily News* saw cuts in immigration, and the increase in the number of literate English-speaking people, as being important for the newspapers.

The golden era may have seemed in 1927 to be enduring, but that was not to last too much longer.

***

Footnote: In 1932, printers in Butte, Montana, went on strike at the town's two newspapers, *The Montana Standard* and the *Butte Post*. For two weeks, the 40,000 people of Butte were without a newspaper. The editorial staff at each newspaper posted typed bulletins in their windows with brief accounts of the most important news, including results from the Olympic Games in Los Angeles. But here is an astonishing fact as recorded by *Time* magazine: 'Local radio stations, co-operating with the newspapers, made few news announcements. Most (newspaper) publishers in neighbouring cities like-wise refrained from taking advantage of the situation, even rejected new mail subscriptions'. Just imagine!

SO WHERE DID THE INDUSTRY GO WRONG?

For decades, newspaper executives have pointed to a "digital tipping point", when revenues from online would offset lost print sales. Now some in the industry are questioning whether there will ever be a profitable future.

—The Financial Times, 9 February 2016.

LET ME COUNT THE ways. Giving content away free on the internet for all those years would probably have to take first prize. What possessed all those highly paid CEOs, chairmen of the board, managing editors, and circulation directors to do such a damn fool thing? I mean, is it not Business 101 to understand that you do not give your products away free? What we are talking about here is a business that is meant to earn revenue and make profits deciding it need not collect revenue on the very thing—the key product—that produces a profit and pays the bills.

In 2009, former *Time* magazine managing editor Walter Isaacson put his finger on the problem in a piece titled 'How to Save Your Newspaper', pointing out that *Time* co-founder Henry Luce disdained the notion of give-away publications on the grounds that the concept was fundamentally flawed. Luce argued that good journalism required a publication to have as its primary duty its responsibility to its readers, not to its advertisers. 'It is also self-defeating, because eventually you weaken your bond with your readers if you do not feel directly dependent on them for revenue'.

The problem today is that, given the lack of profits from digital advertising, newspapers have become even more dependent on potential readers taking out digital subscriptions.

That said, it does not mean that you cannot offer something free if a new reader *pays* for the actual newspaper—but, again, any such offer has to produce a positive revenue result. Some of the offers being made now to entice readers to sign up for digital subscriptions seem, from first glance, unlikely to produce a revenue windfall. It would not be the first time a newspaper promotion has backfired.

In 1927, in its battle for advertising and readers with the *Denver Post*, the *Rocky Mountain News* (which died in 2009) offered a gallon of gasoline free to anyone placing a want (classified) ad. *The Post* countered by offering two gallons. *The News* raised it to three gallons; the *Post* went to four. The papers' offices were besieged with Denverites posting small classified advertisements, the cost of which was far lower than the value of the gasoline they were given.

And the evidence keeps mounting that newspapers have not harnessed the internet to deliver to their bottom lines. But they keep trying: in May 2015, Facebook partnered with nine content companies, including *The New York Times*. And Jim O'Shea, former editor of the *Los Angeles Times*, echoed Henry Luce when he said that publishers, by getting themselves hooked on the incremental dollars generated by Facebook 'are sacrificing audience for ad revenue, which is what they did to get themselves into trouble,' he was quoted as saying by the Poynter journalism website. 'The newspaper industry got into trouble when they subordinated the interest of their readers to that of their advertisers'. But, he went on to concede, he did not know if the newspaper owners had any choice. Newspapers may be faced with the choice between dying on their feet or living on their knees.

As was shown in the preface to the book, adequate digital returns remain as elusive as ever. An April 2015 report by the Pew Research Centre showed that most newspaper content was still being read in print; by contrast, that the average visitor to newspaper websites stayed on average for just three minutes. Moreover, while digital advertising revenue was rising in the United States, it was not growing quickly enough to make up for the fall in print revenue.

Meanwhile, newspapers have dropped the ball in other ways.

What does it tell you when the newspaper industry no longer recruits batches of cadets each year, people who traditionally have been the senior journalists of the future? Very well, the printed form of the newspapers may be going to disappear but someone is going to have to be able to put quality journalism on the websites ten or twenty years from now. Some long-term planning!

And, while I am on the subject of recruitment, how about some diversity? By that I don't mean colour of the skin or nationality, but socio-economic and educational. Why insist all staff have university degrees? (And, if they must have tertiary qualifications, then it would do journalism a great deal more good for those degrees to be in the sciences, the arts, the law, or anything–anything but a journalism degree.)

Back in the late 1960s, when I headed the reporting team at *The Dominion*, the morning daily in Wellington, New Zealand's capital city, that reporting staff included a eighteen-year-old who had come straight off the family farm after a high school education. He was a born police rounds reporter. That enthusiasm you cannot teach; he learned the skills of writing as he went on, but he already possessed a nose for news and eagerness to unearth good stories for the paper. He was not in the least bit interested in national politics, local government, business or any of the other sectors that fill newspapers every day. He just wanted to stay on police rounds.

Other colleagues had done stints on country papers, from small provincial evening dailies to tri-weeklies, where they learned the basic skills. Apprentices are just as important as graduates in an economy, but that diversity is largely gone from the newspaper industry, and the diversity of social experience gone with it. In fact, those with any university education back in the 1960s were in the minority at newspapers at which I worked; the reporting staff at *The Dominion* consisted of one reporter whose father was a railway worker, another a worker in a car plant. Several, including the author, had been raised in public housing. These were reporters who had rubbed shoulders with almost all strata of society.

(On the other hand, two of the reporting staff at that time went on to have university careers, one as a lecturer in Russian.)

Simon Kuper, a columnist with *The Financial Times*, discussed this issue in March 2016 under the headline 'Journalists need to get out more'. He argued that the hit film *Spotlight*—which dealt with paedophile priests being exposed by *The Boston Globe*—flattered the newspaper industry of today. Every print journalist (including this writer) cheered at the story, but Kuper says (in effect) that we are being delusional. 'Most people distrust us and have stopped buying our products', he wrote.

He went on to say one of the industry's problems is that it rarely reports from areas outside the increasingly narrow perspective and background of reporters; in other words, we just don't write enough about the exurbs and poor provincial towns. Journalists tend to live in the rich big cities, and within the trendier suburbs of those cities—to which this writer also pleads guilty.

'Journalists should spread into the provinces and listen to the ordinary people,' Kuper urges. All well and good in theory. But, if we go back to my previous point about the recruiting policies of newspapers in recent decades, and the demand that those recruits should have done a media degree, the call for reporters to go outside their comfort zones is doomed to failure. Most of them wouldn't know where to begin. Most have been brought up in cities, educated at city universities, and then have gone to work for metropolitan media outlets.

As I have said, I worked for many years for *The Australian*, the national newspaper. There were some people who had come up the old-fashioned way, such as starting out at regional papers like the *Bendigo Advertiser* or the *Kalgoorlie Miner*, but the numbers of such people dwindled over the years, and increasingly applied only to the older generation of journalists (many of whom were the first to feel the axe as staff numbers were reduced). It seems to be a worldwide problem, with Kuper citing 'inside the Beltway' in the case of Washington DC, or writing that France's *Le Monde* 'often reads like a Versailles palace gazette circa 1788, chronicling what courtiers are in favour'.

The problem is that this call for greater regional coverage is no longer feasible: the reductions in news-gathering budgets just do not allow for reporters and photographers to be sent off for a few days to remote parts—mainly because (a) the reporters are needed in the office to keep churning out copy for the website and (b) their numbers, and those of photographers, have been so greatly reduced that harassed section editors are trying to cover all the city stories with smaller teams.

***

New Zealand journalist Karl du Fresne raises another issue, what he calls the 'creeping feminization' of newspapers. He's quick to point out that he does not mean the employment of women in the trade, having worked with many fine and outstanding female journalists. Karl du Fresne has been in the business for more than forty years, was editor of the Wellington morning newspaper *The Dominion* (now *The Dominion Post*) and these days writes as a freelance for a range of dailies and magazines.

No, he's talking about the 'increasing proportion of newspaper space devoted to "soft" fluffy human interest stories, gossipy items and lifestyle-oriented content better suited to women's magazines. In metropolitan papers, especially, café reviews and profiles of celebrity chefs, fashion designers, baristas and TV personalities have displaced investigative reporting and traditional "hard" news about events and issues of importance'.

He is, of course, writing about New Zealand papers. Perhaps they have gone too far down that road, and it is not a charge you could level against newspapers everywhere; certainly not the august French newspapers. When it does occur, in many instances, this softer material turns up in specific lifestyle sections and, where *they* exist, colour magazine inserts, and are quite separated from the news and serious feature content. Nonetheless, du Fresne has a point: there is no use trying to duplicate what magazines are doing, if for no other reason than they are failing too, either fading gradually as their circulations dip lower year by year or being closed down completely. And, after all, you could level the same argument about women's magazines. *McCall's*, which in 1968 had a circulation of 8.5 million up until the middle of the twentieth century (*Ladies Home Journal* managed to sell 6.8 million copies of each edition at that time), published serious non-fiction articles and stories by some of America's top fiction writers, along with the fashion and recipes.

And one needs to remember that London's *Daily Mirror* began life in 1903 as the 'paper for gentlewomen'; it was a disaster, with circulation plunging as low as 24,000 before a male editor was put in charge and the content changed to feature photojournalism and more sensational stories.

That 'gentlewoman's' newspaper concept was Alfred Harmsworth's bright idea; he thought existing newspapers did not cater for women readers, and that these women were a vast, untapped pool of readership. It was not as if Harmsworth was a neophyte in the newspaper business; after all, he was the founder of the amazingly successful *Daily Mail*. But women did not want to buy new his new product and men would not be seen reading a 'feminine' product.

However, this is not say that you cannot have offbeat, lighter pieces—what some call 'the sugared pill'; the theory for many editors is that, if you run a lighter photo feature, you hope that readers will also take time over a more serious story placed next to it.

Here is another point, also from New Zealand. In 2016 it was proposed to merge the two newspaper chains (both foreign-owned) that dominated the country's daily newspaper scene, one controlling Auckland's morning paper the *New Zealand Herald* and several provincial afternoon papers and the other owning the morning papers in the capital city, Wellington (*The Dominion Post*) and *The Press* of Christchurch, the South Island's largest city, as well as its own stable of provincial dailies. The ownership issue does not concern us here, because newspaper mergers have become commonplace. No, it was another issue, one highlighted by the country's weekly magazine covering current affairs and the arts (as well as running the television programme schedules), *The New Zealand Listener*. It pointed out that the two groups also operated two of the most read websites in New Zealand, and complained that both those websites were dominated by click-bait, which it defined as ephemeral stories written to excite the casual browser. The magazine's editorial continued thus: 'And while occasional efforts are still made to produce journalism of substance and quality, the change in editorial priorities is reflected in the preponderance of inconsequential human-interest and lifestyle-oriented content'. So it's not just the papers doing it, but the newspaper websites as well that are affecting the image of what newspapers are all about. Take a look any day at the website for one of London's more serious mastheads, *The Daily Telegraph*. Its website has, mixed with its own news and features, 'sponsored content' pushing some commercial interest.

Du Fresne is on firmer ground with his next point: the futility of trying to woo younger readers. The young will not read the newspaper–and you will not get them to read the newspaper's website either, in all probability. It is worth keeping in mind, too, that in some parts of the Western world, literacy standards are falling in many schools, evidenced by the fact that students can end up at a tertiary institution and can barely string a sentence together on paper. That and the 140-character tyranny have resulted in a generation that is not trained to concentrate on anything written at length and in depth.

***

Something interesting has happened in the United States so far as newspaper sales are concerned: single-copy sales are fast disappearing. No longer is it possible for a front page to tempt large numbers of people to impulse-buy a paper. For one thing, they may well have heard the paper's front-page news the previous night or first thing that morning on radio or television. If they had, they have already checked out the story online, long before they walk past a newsstand.

Between 2011 and 2014, the *Des Moines Register* saw a fifty-three per cent decline in single-copy sales, triple the loss that newspaper suffered in home delivery sales.

In May 2016 a study by the Pew Research Centre found that sixty-two per cent of Americans access news on social media, while just over forty per cent get most of their news on Facebook. Why reach into your pocket or purse for some coins to buy a paper when you can just look down at your screen that you carry wherever you go? (Another reason for newspapers–however late in the day it is for them–to go back to scratch and reinvent themselves if they can; the present 'business-as-usual, put a splash on page one and everything else will take care of itself' approach cannot be made to work in this new era.)

Of course, this single-copy sales problem may be peculiarly American. In Australia, for example, a good chunk of the daily print run of a newspaper is grabbed from the local newsagent, or the stall at the suburban railway station. Back in the 1960s and 1970s there were paperboys delivering to the door. Now, in the street where I live (in Sydney, Australia) just one house in a two-block section gets a daily newspaper delivered. So, at least in this part of Sydney, most sales are through local newsstands; on Saturdays, particularly, you have to queue to hand over your money for your newspaper selection (and we are fortunate still to have four local titles from which to choose, plus the locally-printed edition of London's *The Financial Times*).

But getting back to the underlying point: the weakening of the impulse buy and its replacement by the immediacy of electronics is one issue that may not be reversible.

***

And then there is the content—and type of content.

In 1988, in what was clearly a malaise more pronounced in France than in either Britain, Germany or the United States, the Paris papers between them sold 2.7 million copies a day, but that represented all of seventy per cent of newspaper sales across France.

Apart from the stiff competition offered by television and a great profusion of magazines, *The Economist* in 1988 identified the root of the problem besetting French journalism. 'It prefers opinion to facts, and has little taste for investigation. Worse, its opinions are for the most part neither original nor provocative. Many of the Parisian dailies are glaringly partisan,' the magazine reported.

On one level, this is a charge not fairly laid at many papers outside France; they do have original and sometimes provocative articles. On another level, this is a problem in terms of papers being partisan and predictable. In Australia, many conservatives have deserted the Fairfax dailies because of what is seen as left-wing bias. Once upon a time, the *Sydney*

Morning Herald and Melbourne's *The Age* were run as conservative papers by conservative owners. No longer is that the case. Indeed by the later decades of the twentieth century *The Age* was commonly referred to (because of its location in Melbourne) as 'the Spencer Street soviet'.

Here's the point: the old standard of ensuring a clear distinction between news and opinion no longer seems to exist in many newspapers. Moreover, while they might try and separate the two, their news coverage is informed with either conservative or liberal constructs. I spent the early years of my career working for newspapers that supported the conservative side of politics. Many of the journalists were then, as they are now, of a left-ish persuasion. But the news was the news: the management set the agenda and as a reporter you filed stories that were factual and, for want of a better term, straight up and down. In some newspapers, this tight rein has been abandoned.

This really is a short-term type of thinking. Why alienate a great chunk of your potential clientele—you know, people who will actually pay to buy your product?

WHO'S MINDING THE SHOP?

The function of the press in society is to inform, but its role in society is to make money.

—A. J. Liebling, legendary columnist with *The New Yorker*

IN JULY 2011, WHEN reporting on the latest developments at *Le Monde*, *The Economist* reminded its readers that, when the Parisian newspaper had introduced computers to the paper's print works in the early 1990s, the management had hoped to reduce costs through greater production efficiency. By that time, it was common practice for journalists in newspapers around the world to type their copy into the system, and typesetters had become redundant to the newspaper business. But the trades union representing the Paris printers had other ideas: they (successfully) demanded that, for each new computer, *Le Monde* should pay for one print worker to type on the keyboard and another simultaneously to watch the screen as a check system. You just don't know whether to laugh or cry.

Fortunately, in Britain, Rupert Murdoch was minding the shop. (Disclosure: I was employed by Murdoch's *The Australian* newspaper 1988-2007 as a business writer and I continued as a contributor columnist until 2016, so probably will be assumed, to use a deprecatory appellation, to be 'a Murdoch hack'. So be it.)

It was Murdoch who made possible the breaking of the union stranglehold on British newspapers, the so-called 'Spanish practices' that had prevented new technology being introduced and manning levels reduced. The writing was already on the wall for Fleet Street; by the late 1970s the *Daily Mirror's* circulation of more than five million achieved in the early 1960s was but a memory. In 1978 the then owner of *The Times*, Lord Thomson, had spent £3 million on computerized typesetting, but the unions would not allow it to be used. The result was that *The Times* and *The Sunday Times* went unpublished between 1 December 1978 and 13 November 1979 (in the three months before this long closure, there had been twenty-one occasions on which a labour dispute disrupted operations and curtailed the print run).

The attitude of the unions was summed up by a report in March 1979 quoting an official of the National Graphical Association: 'The bosses of *The Times* are on the run. We'll soon be back at work—on our terms'. The union miscalculated when it come to Thomson's resolve.

Eventually a compromise was reached, but mamagement did not prevail entirely and the company suffered a £40 million blow due to the shutdown. Then in 1980 the journalists went on strike, demanding a twenty-one per cent pay rise.

An exhausted Thomson sold out to Murdoch in 1981. By 1986 most Western newspapers had moved to offset printing, but Fleet Street was still stuck in the hot metal, linotype era. Secretly Murdoch built a new, modern printing plant in the London suburb of Wapping, did a deal with a union then outside the newspaper business, and sprang his trap. More than 6,000 workers went on strike but it was too late. The grip of the unions on newspapers had been broken.

And it goes from the ridiculous to the sublimely ridiculous, as *The New York Times* reported in November 2014. At the *Orange County Register*, which had struggled through layoffs and misguided expansions, the delivery of the newspaper was interrupted after the company failed to pay the *Los Angeles Times* for that service. In November, reporters and other employees at the Register were asked to field phone calls from irate customers who didn't receive their papers, as part of a 'We Care' initiative. The paper reported that employees who made twenty calls over two days became eligible to win 'four Maine lobsters, fresh steamers and New England clam chowder'.

You have to know this business: having the desire to run a newspaper is not enough; knowing how every part of the operation runs, something which I suspect is rare in most of the bigger news organizations, is vital. Gardner Cowles could teach today's newspaper executives a thing or two. He was school superintendent in the small Iowa town of Algona; the population was then about 3,800. But it supported two weekly newspapers. He took a half interest in one of them, *The Algona Republican*, and began learning the ropes. He gave that up in 1884 to join his father, who owned the local bank. By 1900 the son, Gardner Cowles, had a controlling interest in ten Iowan banks. In 1903 an old friend persuaded him to buy *The Des Moines Register & Leader*, then up for sale. Only after he sealed the purchase did Cowles find out the true facts about the newspaper, and it was a shock: it was carrying $180,000 in debt had a circulation of just 14,000. He tried to unload the newspaper, but no buyer was found. Cowles had no option but to throw himself into the business and make a go of it. He fired the circulation manager and took over the job himself, making a priority of getting the newspaper into subscriber's hands as soon as possible. He familiarized himself with every small town in Iowa and memorized railway timetables to make sure papers were on the earliest possible train in each direction so that the early editions of the paper were delivered throughout Iowa early each morning; until then readers outside Des Moines received their paper through the mail, obviously not on the day of publication; within ten years, half the paper's circulation (by then 55,000) was outside Des Moines. Then he set about improving the paper, adding a colour comics section to the Sunday edition. He then bought out the afternoon title, the *Des Moines Evening Tribune*; following that he absorbed the other daily, the *Des Moines Capital*. By the mid 1930s, the *Register* had 254 correspondents throughout the state and was delivering about 250,000 copies each morning, including to 72,000 farms.

Circulation reliability is a real problem. For a few months in early 2015, the readers in Sydney of London's *The Financial Times* were able to buy the Saturday edition (the Australian publishing of the weekday editions of that paper had ceased the previous year) not on Saturday mornings, which had long been the norm; no, some weeks the papers made it to the newsagents by mid-afternoon Saturday, and then it became Sunday morning. A daily newspaper being delivered a day late: quite a plan in the twenty-first century. By autumn, however, we were back to Saturday mornings, but what damage had been done in the interim? My local newsagent told me that as the delayed deliveries persisted he had halved his order of the paper.

***

IDEAS THAT MIGHT JUST KEEP NEWSPAPERS GOING —AT LEAST FOR A LITTLE LONGER THAN EXPECTED

In 2010 an estimated 2.3 billion people read a daily paper, twenty per cent more people than were using the internet. In 2010, 200 new daily newspapers came into being.

–World Associations of Newspaper and News Publishers

HOW IS IT POSSIBLE to save newspapers? Answer: it probably is not possible for many titles, especially the mediocre ones, but it is (very) possible to *extend* their lives. This does not apply to those media companies that have, in effect, already thrown in the towel. However, let me differentiate here between companies. Almost all newspaper owners in the developed world have embraced the digital age. They probably did not have much choice. But then the industry splits between those who have decided that print will go soon and are giving that development a helping hand (usually by cutting costs and staff with what appears to be overly much enthusiasm and relish) and those companies that are doing their best to put off the evil day for as long as possible.

That is what this book is about. It is also a riposte to the great many pundits who have solutions to the problems in which newspapers find themselves; however, those 'solutions' almost invariably involve anything but saving the print side of the business and instead offer ideas for better whizz-bang electronic applications.

One solution–if not for the newspaper as a product but for the publishing company that owns the title–is to buy classified property websites, thus clawing back the revenue lost when property advertising deserted print for the web. As *The Financial Times* has noted, in 2003 newspapers got ninety-three per cent of property advertising in the United Kingdom; a decade later the proportion had halved, but most British newspaper groups did not find a way to claw back the lost revenue. In Germany the Axel Springer group, publishers of *Bild* and *Die Welt* dailies, and Norway's Schibsted, which owns several newspapers of which the largest is Oslo-based tabloid *Verdens Gang* did have the presence of mind to acquire property websites. In Australia, Fairfax Media has Domain; in the financial results for the six months ending December 2015, Domain's revenues leapt by seventy-four per cent, eclipsing the performance of the company's print assets. In fact, the total worth of Fairfax's newspapers were put at about half that of its real estate business.

But is also interesting to note other ways in which newspapers are coping with the digital challenge. In 2015, Norway's *Verdens Gang* had a print circulation of 112,716, while there was an online readership of 1.9 million. While the revenues were moving in digital's direction, print still paid the piper. In 2012, *Verdens Gang* produced operating revenues of 1.43 billion krona; that was down to Kr 1.33 billion in 2013, not too great a fall by newspaper industry standards in these times. Online revenue was growing, from Kr 454 million in 2012 to Kr 586 million a year later but, as you can see, still having a long way to go before taking up the slack from print. However, what is also interesting is that the Norwegian paper saw advertising revenues fall by ten per cent over those two years. Weekday circulation of the newspaper fell by thirteen per cent and Sunday circulation by eleven per cent. But sales revenue did not fall as much as that from advertising, it seems, because the paper hiked its cover price, reducing the revenue loss from sales of copies of the paper by only six per cent, while operating costs of producing the print editions fell by five per cent. So that at least was one newspaper not bleeding to death before our eyes.

***

So-called saviour it might be, but online newspapering is not exactly a refined art. Who is not driven made by the advertisements that start screaming in your ear without your needing to click on them? Or the website being slow, or even down? And what about those newspapers that simply do not update often enough? You know, where the top stories are the same at noon as they were when you logged on at 6.30 a.m.

Just take these reader comments. They were appended to an article in *The Australian* written by that newspaper's recently retired editor-in-chief. The column in question could be summed up by the headline: 'News for premium publishers is optimistic'. It was arguing that digital could work financially if the content was good enough. I don't argue with that, as the record of some papers (*The Wall Street Journal* among them) supports that view. In this case the column stated that weekday digital subscriptions had reached 77,371 and print sales Monday to Friday at a 'relatively stable' 101,980.

But let the readers have their say.

'I agree (with an earlier post) that *The Australian* website is not easy to operate or find content. Why have they removed the Business Spectator website which I found very easy to use, and replaced it with a clone of The Australian website?' This poster also noted that 'they make it easy to sign up and ultra-difficult to cancel'. Another reader complained that 'there is so much content in the paper edition that is not featured online – that is, effectively hidden'. (And I would argue from the opposite direction that buyers of the print product have all the additional online content 'hidden' from them even after paying three dollars for a paper.)

A reader called Bernard wrote that the paper's website worked better on a browser on his phone, adding that 'I un-installed the app which I have always thought was limited if not useless'. Laurence, though, was perfectly happy, saying 'I am glad the paywall is working as I would hate to see the demise of a great news service'. Patrick said he had cancelled his subscription to Melbourne's *The Age* 'because of its click-bait, trashy journalism'. (He also raises the point that it was easy get around *The Age's* paywall 'which indicates to me the incompetence of the company'. I would add that it has been relatively easy to get around other newspaper paywalls, too.) But Patrick was satisfied with the quality of *The Australian* content.

But Dennis thought it all cost too much. When he first subscribed the cost was 'A$11 plus change for four weeks. This has rapidly gone to A$16, A$24 and now A$32 ... We are told numbers of subs are increasing, so why the outrageous regular price hikes? As mentioned by others here, the technical standard of the service is pretty poor. Apart from the news, one of my interests is the crossword. As I write, *The Times* (of London, owned by the same company) cryptic is unavailable.' And Raymond grumbled that he went back to look at the former editor-in-chief's article again but it had been taken down. 'What a waste of time'.

This is just one newspaper site taken at random. But, clearly, readers can get very grumpy with technical difficulties. (And here is one of my own: I subscribed to a London paper until, one day, I could not log in. The response from the help desk in London was to tell me that they had been having problems with the newest version of Safari—which I was using—and could I please switch to another browser. Excuse me? How can you run a subscription service that can't cope with some browsers? I cancelled; too much trouble.)

***

I happen to live around the other side of the world from Europe and between twelve and fifteen hours ahead of the main North American cities. It has astonished me that people editing newspapers here have not tumbled to this realization that things can change between press time and the papers hitting in the street.

What I mean by that is illustrated by the financial pages: when I was a daily business reporter, I would dread being asked to write about the latest developments in, for example, the gold price. This request would usually follow a sudden rise or fall of the gold price in New York the previous day (which was overnight in Sydney); so I would trot out a piece explaining the fall/rise and then dread waking the next morning to see the edition with my report hitting the streets at almost exactly the same time as New York closed with the gold price either recovering or collapsing, making my efforts a nonsense.

In May 2016 there was great interest in the elections for a new president of Austria. The count of ballots cast had left the result in the 'too close to call' category. The next morning I picked up the newspaper here in Sydney to read the report on this, which began: 'Austria and the European Union were on tenterhooks last night as they waited to see whether Norbet Hofer had won an election runoff to become the bloc's first president from the anti-immigrant far right'. Well, by the time the newspaper arrived on Sydney doorsteps neither Austria nor the European Union were still on tenterhooks; the postal votes had tipped the election by a whisker to Norbet's left-wing rival.

You know, the really silly thing here is that this type of reporting was not only outdated in the age of the internet, was also made to look irrelevant in earlier decades by radio news. But to run that type of report when anyone turning on the computer first thing in the morning would have been able to see an updated account is simply a waste of newsprint space.

But this type of outdated editing occurs not only when there are considerable differences in time zones.

Newspapers in some countries—India is the leading example—are thriving, many papers recording increased circulations. But Indians do not have the same access to electronic devices that those in the wealthy west do. The newspaper, for many Indians, is the first port of call for the latest news developments.

But in the Western developed nations, why buy a newspaper (unless, of course, you are a technophobe)? Michael Stephens, in his recent book *Beyond News: The Future of Journalism*, goes to the nub of the issue. Sit down at your breakfast table, he writes, with a muffin and a newspaper. The muffin's contents will (or should) be fresh; but the newspaper's contents are anything but. Stephens cities the case of the United States Supreme

Court's decision not to block the healthcare plan designed by President Barack Obama. The decision was on television screens in less than half an hour after its release, and then discussed on radio, television, on blogs, on newspaper websites. Few people interested would not have known about the decision within hours. Yet, next morning, and twenty hours later, the major dailies were hitting the streets with headlines announcing the court's decision as if it were the first the average potential buyer would have known of that decision. Stephens adds: 'The first report you encounter of some intriguing piece of news will almost inevitably be compelling, the fourth not so much'.

I have a more recent example. In June 2016 an Islamic gunman murdered forty-nine people at a gay club in Orlando, Florida. That story broke here in Sydney late afternoon. Before the newspapers hit the streets more than twelve hours later, anyone interested could have tuned in to radio news, then watched local television news; in addition they could have examined streaming news in the internet, while international news channels available on pay-television were providing wall-to-wall coverage.

Of course, twelve hours later the newspapers had to have the story on their front pages. Yes, but did those front-page splashes need to announce that there had been the killings? We all knew that; what was needed was some advance on the actual facts, the indication that the paper was going tell readers something they did not already know. They failed. The paper I bought, *The Australian*, devoted its first six broadsheet pages to the outrage. I just skimmed the headlines: I had seen extensive television coverage, and I had read all the usual websites for details. I did not need another six broadsheet pages rehashing all that was known.

***

I have a few ideas that might just keep newspapers in business for a while longer than many in the industry think possible. In many cases, these involve going back to some of the old ways. But, I hasten to add, in a new context. In this book I have argued a case that, on the one hand, we have forgotten some of the rudiments of what makes a newspaper but, on the other hand, we have stayed too long with the *shape* of what makes a newspaper; in other words, what if we downsized both the structure and the readership of newspapers, so they worked on a totally new economic level (call that a paradigm if you wish)?

The quotation at the head of this chapter is, as you will know, somewhat misleading. Newspapers in the developing world are doing just fine, especially in India, as more people become literate but still cannot afford computers, iPads, and so on. The situation looks somewhat gloomier in mature newspaper markets, but I do not think we should throw in the towel just yet.

You see, I think newspapers have lost their way in terms of content. Ah ha, there is the key word: content. The hardest part of the business and, from the look of many papers not being addressed by those who edit and write them, is re-thinking the approach to content. I am not talking about the daily news list, but the philosophy behind the making of those news lists.

Next question: who the hell do I think I am trying to be heard on this subject? I am not a journalism school professor, and certainly do not have a degree in journalism (which, anyway, did not exist in my country when I started out in this craft). I have never been editor of a newspaper (although I did make it to deputy editor once). I won a journalism prize in 1968 (for investigative reporting) but nothing since (not that I ever entered again). Never worked on Fleet Street or in New York.

Except I never went into public relations, I never went off and worked as a press agent; no, I just kept being a newspaper reporter. Started in 1962, worked daily rounds until 2007 (with detours into books, free-lance journalism and radio and television, although with the two last ones these involved news reporting in the main—indeed, this included a stint at a country radio station where I was the sole news person, responsible for five local bulletins a day and contributing to the hourly national service). My newspaper past (in sequence) includes *The Dominion*, the morning paper in the New Zealand capital of Wellington, a few unhappy months on *The Age* in Melbourne (a paper that was not a good fit for me as I soon discovered), the *South China Morning Post* in Hong Kong in the 1960s, back to *The Dominion* and then its new Sunday offshoot, the awkwardly named *The Dominion Sunday Times*. Next stop was *The Herald*, the broadsheet afternoon title in Melbourne (it would last only into the 1980s), followed by *The National Times*, a weekly published out of Sydney that took itself very seriously. I found a more relaxed atmosphere at *The Australian*, the national daily, with which I have been associated since the mid-1980s.

I stayed in print until 2016 via a weekly mining company column in *The Australian*. Since this column became the victim of another round of budget cuts, my journalism income is derived from the electronic media in the form of websites in Perth and Toronto for which I write each week.

Perhaps this book is just another triumph of hope over expectation but, frankly, it breaks my heart to see the newspaper industry in its present state. I was in this business for fifty-four years (with, as mentioned, some detours into radio and television and books). Pick up a book on newspapers and journalism today and the chances are it has been written by a journalism academic. What you are now reading is, by contrast, a report from someone who has spent more than half a century doing the hard graft of finding stories, researching them, and writing them. Moreover, reading newspapers is still one of the great joys of my life—provided the newspaper is any good. And, I regret to add, too many newspapers are not all that good anymore.

But let us not give up. Not just yet.

***

In 2015 the *Toronto Star* did something amazing: it decided to find ways to make more money out of its print product. This followed the failure of its attempt to maintain a paywall. The paper found that, on introducing that paywall, it had ninety days of good growth. Then subscriptions plateaued. Then costs began rising for every subscription gained and churn rates grew. The paywall died and the newspaper (Canada's biggest) told its readers 'the decision to cancel Digital Access means readers will receive full access to thestar.com, including all the news articles, columnists, investigative reports, sports, multimedia features and much more that combined make the *Toronto Star*, in print and online, the best and most comprehensive provider of news and information in Canada'.

They should have known what to expect. Back in 2013 online readership at the city's other newspaper, the *Globe and Mail*, saw its online readership plummet by forty per cent after it introduced a paywall.

The *Star* then actually tried to find out what its readers wanted by doing extensive market research. One of those things included better television program listings. You see, much of what newspapers do is mundane, but if you are still of a mind to buy a physical newspaper each day then television listings is one of those features you want there every day.

Here is another problem for most players building a digital news product: your potential audience may not be all that large. It is one thing for *The Wall Street Journal, The Financial Times* or *The New York Times* (and many others such as the *South China Morning Post*, because of its Chinese coverage) because they cover the world, and people throughout the world want to read what they present. That is borne out by the fact that those papers actually print in more than one region; you can pick up *The International New York Times* (the rebranded *International Herald Tribune*, rebranded wrongly in my view given that paper's name recognition and high standing) each day in Paris, for example, or in Tokyo as an insert in *The Japan Times*, or in many other cities.

But if you run a small city newspaper, or a small town one, how much upside is there for an online audience, especially one with enough people to pay to view your site? Homesick home-towners might like to keep in touch, but otherwise your website is just going to cannibalize your print sales.

***

'Newspapers Strive to Win Back Women' was a headline in *The Wall Street Journal* on 4 May 1992. Over the previous twenty years, the *Journal* reported, more women than men had stopped reading metropolitan dailies. By 1992, however, some of the large chains–such as Knight-Ridder, Thomson and Scripps Howard–were trying to win back women. For example, the *Chicago Tribune* had in 1991 introduced a 'Womanews' section complete with classified advertisements aimed at women. In many papers, a distinct women's section made a comeback. Other strategies included beefing up coverage of issues such as day care. But Knight-Ridder also did some market research, and found women complaining that papers had material that was badly aimed: for example, fashion sections that featured clothes that were too expensive or food sections that had far too complicated recipes and that working women did not have time to prepare. The *Journal* noted that women's sections had been eliminated by 'news-room feminists' in the 1970s; before that, they had typically carried practical features on issues that were the everyday concerns of many women—sewing, cooking, tea parties and marriage.

This does not contradict the point made by Karl du Fresne earlier about the 'feminization' of newspapers. There is quite a difference between soft features and practical information addressing the everyday concerns of women. Perhaps, however, we can forget tea parties and sewing in these modern times, and address issues that concern women (both stay-at-homes and working ones) in the twenty-first century. But do address them.

But recipes, yes, please. (Men like them too.) Simple things are probably best, in contrast to the many cookbooks that frighten the life out of all but the most redoubtable cook. A feature with recipes under the headline 'Healthy Food Your Kids Will Love' would be a godsend to any newspaper.

But are there not enough women's magazines that do this sort of thing? Well, yes, but we are not talking here about saving magazines, but newspapers. Moreover, newspapers in the 1930s ran plenty of recipes and that was an era of burgeoning women's magazine titles. Here is one I came across in *The Washington Post*:

Mushroom Barley soup (1932)

2 tbsp of coarse barley
½ cup fresh mushrooms
1 onion
3 carrots
1 stalk celery
1 tbsp of butter
1 tbsn of flour
4 cups of vegetable stock

Soak the mushrooms for an hour and then boil them with the barley until tender. Then drain. Add chopped onion, carrot and celery. Brown the butter and flour, blend, and then add to the soup mixture. Add all the vegetable stock into saucepan or soup pot, then add the vegetable-barley mixture. Simmer gently on low heat for 1 hour.

You could make that today, and it sounds quite healthy and tasty (and easy to make after a day at work).

Newspapers need to make themselves more useful, and provide practical information—a service most of them long ago abandoned. If you read a newspaper today and are looking for food ideas, it is most likely that it will be restaurant reviews, or the 'ten best chicken restaurants in X (insert your city's name)'. It is interesting to note that one of the most successful magazines, *Hello!*, contains a recipes section, and recipes that are relatively easy to make. Yes, you can search recipe sites online, but this is time-consuming. If readers are time-poor, and they find themselves clipping recipes from a newspaper, then they will tend to buy the newspaper.

And remember how I earlier referred to *The New York Times* scrapping its movie listing? Just before that, *The Australian* began running such lists—and this involves considerable work because the paper is national; its solution was to just run Sydney listings in the Sydney print run, the Brisbane ones in the paper printed there, and so on. Someone obviously thought it would provide a service to readers. Going online requires time and thought: turning to the specific information page in a newspaper does not.

Pack the pages

One of the great mistakes, in my not so humble opinion, was that newspapers stopped looking jam-packed with stories. This is hard to do if you have gone tabloid, or the long narrow 'broadsheet' adopted widely in North America and elsewhere. But it can be done: I can remember reading copies of London's *Daily Mirror* in the 1950s and marveling at the information that was packed into a news item that might consist of two sentences. Of course, it is probably harder to achieve these days when, so far as I can see, younger journalists become 'writers' rather than practising a craft.

This is what newspapers used to look like:

There's an awful lot there to catch the eye, isn't there? Contrast that with today's newspapers and you would be lucky with many to find more than three items on the front. Those old newspapers gave you the impression that they were just busting with news; today most give the impression that they are just picking a small selection of stories. Warren Buffett has been complaining about this. A newspaper owner among many other things, he remarked in mid-2016 that papers did not tell him as many things as they had even ten years earlier. 'There's less and less in the newspaper', he added. By contrast, I would add, the information available on the internet gives the impression of being infinite.

It was drummed into cadet reporters when I started out in 1962 that you wrote a news report assuming that it could be cut back. So you were taught to write the most important fact in the lead paragraph, the second most important in the second, a third in the third, and so on, so that either the sub-editorial desk could just pull off the last pages of copy paper (we wrote one paragraph per slip so that paragraphs could be shuffled or deleted at will) or whoever was supervising pages being put together on the stone could just have the last (however many) lines needed to be cut removed by the compositor.

This in 1963, this was typical of a news item I wrote as a junior reporter on *The Dominion*, the morning broadsheet in Wellington, the New Zealand capital.

First paragraph: 'Three quarter of Upper Hutt's population could be fully supplied with underground water if use was made of artesian pools in the area, a spokesman for the New Zealand Geological Survey said.' *You would not want to cut there, but could if there was available only a tiny space at the bottom of column for this news.*

Second paragraph: 'He told *The Dominion* the area could draw between three and four hundred million gallons a year, which would satisfy the demands of up to 15,000 people.' *Now you could—again, only if need be—end the item there.*

Third paragraph: 'The Lower Hutt artesian basin has been used for many years as a ground water supply for Lower Hutt, Petone and Eastbourne.' *You see, the story is widened out a little more, but again could be self-contained if terminated at this point.*

The report actually goes on for another seven paragraphs, each adding a little more detail and elaboration, and could be cut anywhere. Now, I am not holding my early work as anything more than run-of-the-mill journalism—and no doubt it had been tidied up a great deal by some veteran sub-editor with a cigarette hanging out of his mouth, and possibly ash fallen on to his cardigan—but here's my point: let's get back to run-of-the-mill journalism. Makes those pages look busy. Watch someone reading a newspaper these days: chances are they will flip over pages with barely a glance at some. They can do that because there these days only a small number of items on a page,

and the subjects of those can be sized up quickly by the reader. Pack those
same pages with more items, and the chances are the reader's eye will be
caught by something. Sure, it involves bruised egos with reporters finding
their precious words chopped, but let us think about the readers first, shall
we?

Go back to mixing up the pages: have your big lead, followed by a few
medium stories in importance, and pack small items around them.

Look at these two images on the previous pages: the initial impression
is of a busy page; you pause to check out all the stories. Today, you can see
the one or three items on a page, know it's not for you, and move on. You
start to see your newspaper as the 'two-minute silence'.

If you have a broadsheet, this busy, busy page need not look a mass
of grey type. Small, one-column illustrations should be used with as many
items as possible, from head shot photos, graphs, maps, and so on. We live
in a visual age, and that does not just mean running one large photograph
on each page. Why has no one thought of this point? Why can't a broadsheet page be as tempting as a busy webpage?

**

Try a new type of paper?

Launching old style newspapers in the modern era has not worked well.
There was *The Sun*, launched in 2002 in New York, using the name and
masthead of one of the city's dead newspapers (the original had been published between 1833 and 1950). The new version was intended to appeal
to readers who wanted an alternative in terms of a serious paper to *The New
York Times*. It did not work financially, and the print edition was closed in
2008, although the title exists online.

In 2004 there was an effort to launch a new London-based daily to be
called *The World*. It was to be modeled on *Le Monde*, and was promoted as
an antidote to what the lead promoter, Stephen Glover, described as 'the
dumbing-down of the broadsheet press'. He said Britain was the only country in the world that did not have an uncompromisingly upmarket title; he
excluded *The Financial Times* because it was not a general newspaper.

Glover had been one of the founders of *The Independent* (which, as we have noted, ceased being available in print in 2016) and has become a commentator on the media. His plan was to aim for a circulation of 100,000. He did not provide further details but clearly the intention of the group was to follow the 'uncompromisingly' seriousness of *Le Monde*. Glover said the goal was to raise £15.4 million.

The proposal never got off the ground. But it did provoke a comment from Andrew Neil, a former editor of *The Sunday Times* and at that time editor of Business (the rebranded weekly newspaper previously known as *The Sunday Business*). He argued that the capital budget for Glover's newspaper was not realistic, pointing out that £40 million had been spent to get *Business* where it was by 2004, and that was a weekly publication, not a daily one.

Most recently we have seen Trinity Mirror, one of the large British newspaper publishers, try and fail to launch a new title. In 2016, its *The New Day* lasted ten weeks. As Ben Nicholson wrote in *The Guardian* when closure was announced, it launched 'with the curious aim of appealing to "normal people" who don't like reading newspapers, and on this point they were absolutely right—normal people didn't want to read this newspaper either'.

One interesting aspect was that the new paper's management decided against a web presence. Moreover, it employed only twenty-five people, so there was none of the traditional over-manning that has been such a burden to the newspaper industry.

Nick Tjaardstra of the World Association of Newspapers commented upon the closure that existing papers had spent decades building an audience. Then he put his finger on the problem: 'The interesting takeaway from *The New Day* is that they probably saw the venture as much less risky than a digital-only pitch where their content would have had no paid value and digital ad revenue would have been low without scale or targeting.'

Indeed.

So what sort of model does work?

Perhaps the one I mentioned near the beginning of this book: an extremely small-scale operation, and perhaps a one-day-a-week one. Many newspapers have, or are planning to, cut back to, say three days a week, or just printing for Saturday sales, the non-printing days being covered by online content. But that seems unsatisfactory in some way, being neither fish nor fowl.

But something needs to be done. Just retrenching staff every year or so does not sound to me much like a business plan.

It is an astonishment to me that so little is being done to rethink the newspaper model.

Perhaps it cannot be done; perhaps, as the pessimists forecast, the newspaper industry is a goner.

But here is another thought, and one that goes back to Stephen Glover's aspiration to produce an 'uncompromising' product. Once newspapers attracted a different sort of writer than those of today do, people who were not what our idea is of a professional journalist—and I make this point even though I am one of those professional journalists.

The British magazine, *The Spectator*, in 1954 ran an article by one John Beavan entitled 'Fleet Street 1954', and one that looked back at pre-war newspapers. 'In the Thirties Fleet Street was still on nodding terms with literature,' he wrote. Many of the noted writers of that era, like G.K. Chesterton and Hillaire Belloc, not only contributed articles to newspapers but were regularly seen drinking at the bars patronized by the professional newspaper writers.

He complained that the nature of newspapers had changed (for the worse) after the war. There were few chances for writers to, well, write; instead articles would be 'butchered' to fit into predetermined spaces on a page. 'That was what killed writing in Fleet Street – that and the knowledge that most of the new readers preferred simple, bright stories lacking any distinction of literary style. Sub-editors, once the mice of Fleet Street, who ticked the caps, and diffidently shortened the wink (the sparkle) of better people, now became bossy re-write men, "processing" the copy, producing pre-digested pap,' he complained.

(Yes, I know, this is a repudiation of my earlier suggestion of 'packing the pages—but perhaps we can have the best of both worlds; a few star 'writers' and then the hacks providing the shorter pieces.)

As this writer can testify, journalism was a lure for many in spite of the generally appalling pay rates. In the late 1970s the British Advisory,

Conciliation and Arbitration agency (usually known as Acas) did a study of English provincial newspapers. In eleven of thirteen provincial publishing groups, compositor wages were higher than those of the journalists. The journalists in those eleven companies earned on average twenty-five per cent less than did what we used to call the Black-Hand Gang.

With some exceptions, this writer's experience is that journalists tended to be employed on sufferance. In one company in the 1990s, you could walk into the office of someone on the business side of the paper and detect a standard of equipment (notably telephones with caller identification screens) that were not provided to the reporters on the newsroom floor (when caller-ID was something they could have found handy). Middle ranking advertising sales people had parking spaces, but not senior reporters. And so on.

Another problem, as diagnosed by Beavan, was that Fleet Street's success had weakened the quality of journalism.

'Since 1939 the (Daily) *Mirror* has found three million new readers, the (Daily) *Express* a million and a half. Many of them did not read a paper at all before the war; they lacked the means and perhaps the desire to do so,' noted. 'But to catch and preserve the interest of these people it has been necessary to dramatise lighter news more heavily than before.' And the more serious of the popular dailies, the *Daily Herald* and *News Chronicle*, had been forced to follow suit.

But, in the early nineteen-fifties, television was becoming the increasingly dominant media. As one commentator at the time put it, 'television flourishes at the expense of traditional journalism. It turns readers into viewers. It gives them the news faster than the press, with a visual impact beyond the power of print. It carries authority, as well as magnetism; the common man's credibility yardstick now is not "I saw it in the paper", but "I saw it on telly".'

At the same time, long-honoured newspaper techniques were losing their potency. Human interest could not be wrung more thoroughly, nor headlines made much bigger. Then, as now, newspapers persevered with old practices long after they were no longer valid, and the readers departed. As they do now.

(After re-reading this section, I can see many contradictions. But there are a number of points that the newspaper industry should consider; it might just be out of this hodge-podge of ideas that a viable idea may be gleaned. After all, the present plan is not working.)

***

Look on your own doorstep

Cover the local scene, and look for the small stories. At the time that news item I cited earlier on underground water appeared, my responsibilities included sitting through the monthly meetings of the Hutt Valley Underground Water Authority, along with meetings of the Petone, Upper Hutt and Eastbourne borough councils, which rarely yielded more than a few paragraphs for the bottom of one of the back news pages; then there were afternoons spent taking notes at meetings of the Hutt River Board, the Hutt Valley Drainage Board, the Lower Hutt City Council and the Hutt County Council. On top of that I covered the two magistrates and coroner courts in the Hutt Valley (part of the greater Wellington area in New Zealand) and made daily (personal not telephone) calls to the local police stations.

When I worked briefly in Melbourne in the 1960s for *The Age*, I did a stint as lower courts reporter. This involved calling around all the suburban courts and finding our from the court clerks what was on that day's dockets, then driving frantically from court to court to try and cover as many as possible of the more interesting cases.

The U.S.-based Medialife website has run some interesting posts on the small-town newspaper sector. Their argument was all to do with the fact that these papers have been less affected by the digital onslaught than the major big city dailies.

The local papers cover the small stories. Take courts: television and radio report on the more spectacular court cases, but there are thousands of cases that would fascinate readers even though they are among the minutiae of daily life. In 1965 this reporter had an eight-sentence item published in the back pages of *The Dominion*. Excuse the reporting protocols of the time, but this was about an unknown young man in a suburban backyard.

FATAL DASH TO AVOID BEE

In an attempt to avoid a bee a youth tripped and died, the Coroner's Court, Lower Hutt, was told yesterday.

The Coroner, Mr L. H. Herd, was inquiring into the death at Lower Hutt of 18-year-old Donald William Wilkie.

Eileen Wilkie, the deceased's mother, said she and her son were feeding birds in a neighbour's back garden. Suddenly Donald called out: 'Look at this bee, it's going to sting me.'

He then started running to avoid the bee. Running up concrete steps to the back door of the house, he appeared to slip and struck his temple on the concrete.

'I went too fast. Give me an aspirin,' Donald said, just before lapsing into unconsciousness.

Douglas Trevor Beetham, resident surgeon at Hutt Hospital, said Wilkie was admitted shortly after the incident. He was unconscious. Three operations were performed over the next 24 hours, but brought about only temporary improvement.

Wilkie remained in a coma until his death more than four weeks later.

The Coroner found that Wilkie died of head injuries following an accidental fall.

One would have written this a little more elegantly today, and improved the construction (as in 'performed over the *following* 24 hours'), but fifty-one years later I find this brief and matter-of-fact report still affecting. But what metropolitan newspaper would cover that hearing these days? Yet I am sure that newspaper readers today would stop and read such a story (if only newspapers would cover such seemingly small but affecting court stories).

If you want to own a newspaper, buy a small town one

The Medialife website looked at small newspapers and how many of them were making money (albeit not as much as they were pre-digital). And we're talking real small here, the website citing the *Chickasha Express Star* in the town of that name in Oklahoma; with a population for the town around 16,000 (although the number would rise if you counted other nearby communities) the paper sold 4,600 copies a day; in Taunton, Massachusetts, there live 56,000 people and *The Taunton Daily Gazette* manages to maintain a circulation of 6,700.

Medialife sets out the advantages of operating small town dailies. They are:

They have deep roots in their communities, covering everything from school board meetings to Little League games.

They enjoy the support of local businesses and can offer affordable advertising rates

They remain print-focused. Sure, they have a website but print is their bread and butter.

They are lean operations; in hard times, they need lay off very small numbers of staff (in other words, no mass sackings like at the major dailies).

They have experienced staffs. Small town papers tend to keep their staff people for a long time, and these people know how the town ticks.

Warren Buffett's Berkshire Hathaway Media group is certainly following this policy. When in early 2015 the company bought two additional dailies, *The Martinsville Bulletin* and the *Franklin News-Post*, Associated Press noted that Buffett had said he thought newspapers would continue to earn a decent return so long as they remained the primary source of information about their communities. In a 2013 letter to shareholders Buffett declared that he believed 'that papers delivering comprehensive and reliable information to tightly bound communities and having a sensible internet strategy will remain viable for a long time.'

Berkshire Hathaway has bought thirty-two dailies, including the *Tulsa World* in Oklahoma, and forty-seven weeklies in Nebraska, New York state, Iowa, Texas, Oklahoma, Virginia, North Carolina, South Carolina, Alabama and Florida.

However, in an interview in late May 2016 with a reporter from *USA Today*, Buffett did reveal that, even for him, being in the newspaper business was no cakewalk. He admitted to not having cracked the code to keep newspapers profitable longer term (his do all make a profit for now, however).

But, I think Buffett is correct when he says that, for newspapers to succeed, they have to be essential—to provide information readers cannot find anywhere else. How many papers can claim they do that well?

***

In New Zealand, newspapers have suffered as everywhere. But some have survived by going local. In fact, for a country with just 4.7 million people, it is astonishing that it supports twenty-two daily newspapers. All but a handful are owned by two large chains, but three of the independently owned ones seem to be holding their own particularly well.

One is the *Otago Daily Times*, located in the South Island city of Dunedin. Its circulation of around 36,000 is said to have remained reasonably stable. Writer Karl de Fresne (a former daily editor himself) three years ago profiled the paper for the national weekly, the *New Zealand Listener*. He found that the paper, owned by two brothers whose family had been in the newspaper business in Dunedin for five generations, had managed an unusually high penetration rate and a high ratio of subscribers as opposed to casual sales. 'It has achieved this through a simple but effective strategy of unabashed parochialism in its editorial content,' wrote de Fresne. 'It's a rare day when the main story on page one isn't local.'

And Allied Press, the company that owns the *Otago Daily Times*, also controls two small papers located on the west coast of the South Island. *The Greymouth Star* publishes six days a week in a town with a population of about 9,500 while, about an hour's drive away, the *Hokitika Guardian* hits the streets six mornings a week in a town with about 3,500 people.

Also in the South Island is the town of Ashburton (pop. 18,500) with an afternoon newspaper, the *Ashburton Guardian*. The paper, owned by a local family, comes out six days a week and sells on average around 5,400 copies a day. The only other newspaper available in the town is the morning *The Press* from Christchurch, which general manager Desme Daniels says is no competition because it has no Ashburton content. She says the paper keeps its content on the first five to seven pages 'hyper-local' and that the staff knows the local paper and what people there want to read about.

It is worth adding that not too many years ago *The Press* had pages devoted to regional news, with correspondents in provincial towns such as Blenheim, Greymouth and Ashburton keeping the residents of those and other areas informed of the local events of note. No more, alas.

***

Here's a twist to the small town newspaper story. The editor of the Vermont weekly *The Hardwick Gazette*, Ross Connelly, gave a speech in 2009 about his newspaper, which now sells about 2,200 copies a week. One point he made was that his newspaper did not have a website. One reason was money; the costs of being on the web would have been a stretch for the paper's budget, and it would have made matters worse by requiring more staff. 'A staff of four full-time people, two part-time people and several correspondents does not give us the time to put the newspaper on the web each week,' he said. 'And we have enough trouble getting local businesses to advertise. I am not convinced they would want to pay extra to have their ads linked to the web pages.' And then there would be the manpower needed to solicit and administer online subscriptions.

And those old copies?

Make money from your archive—or, at least, attract online or print subscribers using the lure of access to the archive. *Time* magazine has done that and I know one person (yes, me) who took out a subscription to *Time* for that privilege; after all, the magazine is a shadow of its former self but I spent hours reading wonderful journalism the news magazine produced all those years ago.

As *The New York Times* opined in 2008, 'publications are rediscovering their archives, like a person learning that a hand-me-down coffee table is a valuable antique'. The report was pegged to the move at that time by *Sports Illustrated* to open up what the paper described as a 'fifty-three-year trove of articles and photos, most of it from an era when the magazine dominated the field of long-form sports writing and colour sports photography'.

Using the archive as a subscriber lure is just one more marketing idea that could be more widely employed.

****

These are just a few random suggestions. Some may work, others may not, or they may all be dismissed as the pipe dreams of a tired old hack. But this tire old hack would love to see newspapers survive. Over to you.

POSTSCRIPT

'The death spiral of print advertising is before us. And I'm an optimist.'

–Ken Doctor, Newonomics

'Publishers are feeding on what is falling off the tech giants' table, but these scraps are becoming increasingly scant: digital ad revenues at The New York Times were lower in the first quarter (of 2016) than they were a year ago.'

–*The Financial Times*, May 2016. The article said that, by contrast, Facebook and Google had captured $20 billion spent on mobile digital ads in 2015.

***

And why you should listen to someone from the newspaper trenches:
'Most of the self-styled teachers of journalism are the worst possible guides, even from a commercial point of view, because they are unable to put their own precepts into practice. If they really knew how to make money out of journalism they would be doing it, instead of selling their secret to others'
George Orwell, Manchester Evening News, 11 January 1945.
This author duly takes note.

***

But, before we end, one last, lingering look back to the way it once was. In 1952, writer E.C. Krauss wrote a piece in the *Los Angeles Times* recalling his days in New York newspapers in the first decade of the twentieth century. In those pre-Great War days, the action was all at City Hall, so newspaper companies located themselves as closely as possible to the epicenter of the city's political action, buying up properties just across the street in Park Row. That section soon became known as Newspaper Row. As Krauss recalls:

> 'When I hit New York in the first decade of the century Newspaper Row was a reality. The *Tribune*, the *Sun*, the *World* were practically next door to each other, the *Times* had only recently moved uptown and the *Press* was just around the corner. Since the *Sun* and the *World* published both morning and evening, that made six newspapers in a single block ... Two more were within hailing distance, the *Hearst Journal* (evening) and *American* (morning) ... As famous as Newspaper Row itself were two beaneries where newspapermen dined frugally the day before payday and sometimes earlier ... On the other side of the Brooklyn Bridge entrance was a well known beer saloon—a block long, since it ran from Park Row to William St.'

BIBLIOGRAPHY

Bogart, Leo, "Newspapers in Transition", *The Wilson Quarterly*, Vol. 6, No. 5 (1982)

Brock, George, Out of Print: Newspapers, *Journalism and the Business of News in the Digital Age*, Kogan Page, London 2013.

Douglas, George H, *The Golden Age of the Newspaper*, Greenwood Publishing 1999

McGilligan, Patrick, Young Orson, *The Years of Luck and Genius on the Path to Citizen Kane*, Harper 2015

Stephens, Michael, Beyond News: *The Future of Journalism*, Columbia University Press 2014.

Throgmartin, Clyde, *The National Daily Press of France*, Summa Publications, 1998.

All other sources used are identified in the text.

INDEX

.

OTHER BOOKS BY ROBIN BROMBY

(and available through Amazon):

<u>Popular history titles</u> (available in e-book format and paperback via Amazon)

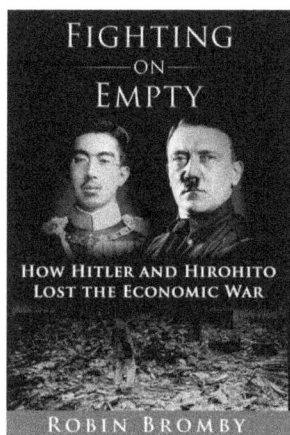

Fighting on Empty: How Hitler and Hirohito Lost the Economic War

Nazi Germany, Imperial Japan and Fascist Italy all embarked on their Second World War plans of conquest without one vital factor: sound economies that could absorb and withstand the stresses of total war. In this groundbreaking study, Robin Bromby shows how all three Axis powers went into battle with seriously flawed economies, inadequate industrial capacity and deficient food security. When they invaded much of Europe and East Asia, the Nazis and their partners only compounded the problem: they had made few plans to manage their conquests and failed to harness captured factories and farms.

It was a fatal flaw: their war plans were doomed. Despite the legend of a beleaguered Britain, that country was the largest economy in Europe and was soon building more aircraft than Germany—and had its empire on which to call. Japan's lack of economic planning was breathtaking and the strains soon began to show. And then came the Americans with all their economic power. The Axis was finished.

Fighting on Empty reveals a largely ignored, but crucial, aspect of the Second World War.

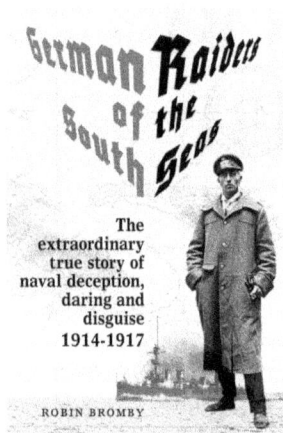

German Raiders of the South Seas: The extraordinary true story of naval deception, daring and disguise 1914-1917.

Far from the mud and slaughter of the Western Front, there was another face of the Great War— an oddly stirring and thrilling one, characterized by chivalry and remarkably few casualties. This is the story of how three German naval surface raiders disrupted British shipping across large swathes of the Indian and Pacific oceans between 1914 and 1917. Attempts to supply critical cargoes and much needed reinforcements for the trenches in France and Belgium were hamstrung by German daring on the high seas.

Were it not all real and true, it would make wonderful fiction: the buccaneering crew of the Emden casting a shadow of fear over an ocean; the survivors of the battle with the Sydney sailing a leaking copra schooner from the Cocos Islands to the East Indies, the captain of the Seeadler, von Luckner, sailing a small boat halfway across the Pacific to Fiji, and then later making a dramatic escape from a New Zealand prisoner of war camp.

In the first days of World War I a German light cruiser detached itself from the East Asiatic Squadron with the mission to raid and harass Allied shipping. The ship, SMS Emden, not only became world famous in its two months of raiding, during which it sank sixteen ships and captured others, but demonstrated the vulnerability of Australian, New Zealand and Empire shipping links.

New Zealand Railways: Their Life & Times

NEW ZEALAND RAILWAYS
Their Life and Times
ROBIN BROMBY

New Zealand railway builders surmounted many obstacles: the terrain, a sparse and scattered population, two islands separated by an often stormy stretch of water, demands from every small settlement for their own railway line. But build a railway system—and a comprehensive one at that—New Zealand did. This is the story of that railway, from its heyday to the day of reckoning as losses had to be confronted.

By 1953 the pattern was clear. The era of railways as the mainstay of land transport throughout New Zealand was ending. One by one, most of the rural branches would disappear over the next forty years; passenger train travel—other than commuter services in Auckland and Wellington—would almost disappear to a stage where there are just a handful of tourist services on the most scenic lines; all but the largest towns would lose their railway station.

But, until then, the railways of New Zealand were part of almost everyone's life: you caught the train to visit friends and relatives in other parts of New Zealand, you depended on the trains to carry the bulk of the freight that moved to and from the ports. This is their story. Profusely illustrated with photographs and maps.

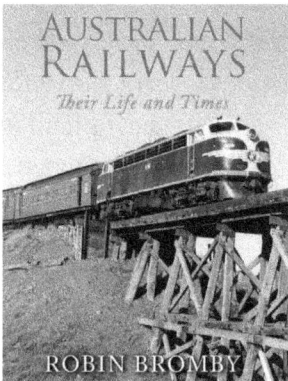

Australian Railways: Their Life and Times

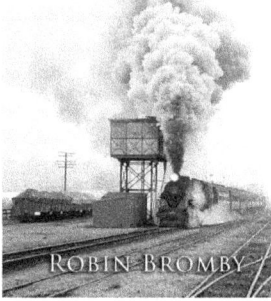

AUSTRALIAN RAILWAYS
Their Life and Times
ROBIN BROMBY

The nightmare of three different gauges, the daunting challenge of building railways across vast open spaces often with no water supplies, the follies of railway lines that were rarely used—all this is the saga of Australian railways, the sheer hard work and suffering of those who gave their life in service to the railways. Brimming with anecdotes and colorful stories, *Australian Railways: Their Life and*

Times documents the old, the odd and the now forgotten. Complete with rare historic photographs.

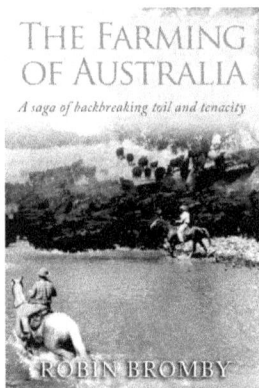

The Farming of Australia: A saga of backbreaking toil and tenacity

This is the story of triumph over a dry, hot and often infertile land. Australia's farmers have overcome difficult terrain and the tyranny of distance to make the country an important food bowl. This is the story of 200-plus years of ups and downs from savage droughts and daunting challenges to the triumphs of irrigation and imagination and inventiveness.

Business and Resources titles (in e-book format only)

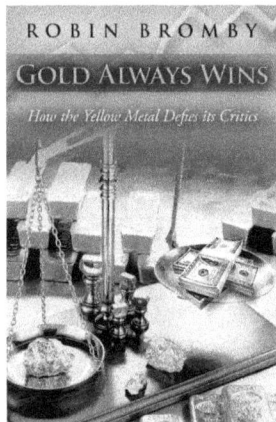

Gold Always Wins: How the Yellow Metal Defies its Critics

Why do so many people try to diminish the gold story? And why does gold keep bouncing back in defiance of its critics? That is the theme of this book: that gold's fundamental appeal—as a safe haven, the ultimate store of wealth, the most reliable form of money—sees it through every obstacle put in its way. In the past 100 years, the world has turned its back on the gold standard (and in the case of the U.S. actually banned its private ownership) and developed a multitude of new financial tools through the use of derivatives and massive leveraging, and yet gold is still at the beating heart of the global financial system.

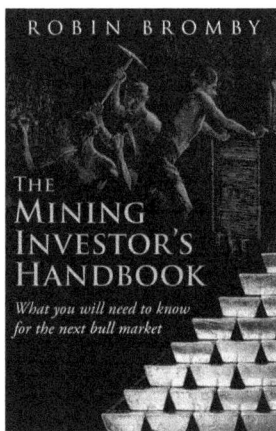

www.ingramcontent.com/pod-product-compliance
Lightning Source LLC
La Vergne TN
LVHW091311080426
835510LV00007B/470

9 780099 259564 7